Watching Yellowstone & Grand Teton Wildlife

By Todd Wilkinson
Photography by Michael H. Francis

RIVERBEND
PUBLISHING

Dedication

For Carter and Natalie

Photo Identification:
    Page 1: Trumpeter swans
    Page 3: Bobcat
    Page 4: Bighorn sheep
    Page 6: Bald eagle
    Page 12-13: Gray wolves
    Page 18-19: Bison

Copyright © 2004 Riverbend Publishing
Text © Todd Wilkinson
Photographs © Michael H. Francis

Published by Riverbend Publishing, Helena, Montana

Printed in South Korea

4 5 6 7 8 9 0 SI 09 08 07

ISBN 1-931832-27-7

Cataloging-in-Publication data is on file at the Library of Congress.

Riverbend Publishing
P.O. Box 5833
Helena, MT 59604
1-866-787-2363
www.riverbendpublishing.com

About the Author and Photographer

Author Todd Wilkinson has been writing about wildlife in Yellowstone and Grand Teton national parks since the mid-1980s. He is a western correspondent for *The Christian Science Monitor* and a regular contributor to more than a dozen magazines, including *Audubon, Outside,* and *Orion.* In addition to this book, he has written eight others, including *Watching Glacier's Wildlife, Rocky Mountain National Park: A Wildlife Watcher's Guide, Grand Canyon-Zion-Bryce National Parks: A Wildlife Watcher's Guide, Track of the Coyote,* and *Bison for Kids.*

Photographer Michael H. Francis worked seasonally in Yellowstone National Park for 15 years before becoming a full-time wildlife photographer. His fine work has been published by the National Geographic Society, the Nature Conservancy, the Audubon Society, the National Wildlife Federation, and *Field & Stream, Outdoor Life,* and *Natural History* magazines, among others. He has photographed more than a dozen books, including *Watching Glacier's Wildlife; Rocky Mountain National Park: Into the Wind: Wild Horses of North America: Mule Deer Country; Wild Sheep Country;* and *Elk Country.*

Acknowledgments

In particular, the author extends warm thanks to former Yellowstone research specialist Norm Bishop, park ornithologist Terry McEneaney, and Yellowstone's former assistant chief ranger Gary Brown for graciously reviewing the manuscript and offering valuable suggestions. Appreciation also is directed toward the National Park Service, U.S. Fish and Wildlife Service, and U.S. Forest Service for the information those agencies supplied. As always, Yellowstone's chief spokesperson Marsha Karle and her staff have provided crucial access to park officials and information. Thanks, too, are in order to Yellowstone research chief John Varley and to technical writer Paul Schullery for their insight and patience over the years. In addition, appreciation is accorded the Yellowstone Institute, Grand Teton National History Association, Northern Rockies Conservation Cooperative based in Jackson, Wyoming, Teton Science School, and the Greater Yellowstone Coalition. Without the help of all of these people and institutions, completion of the book would not have been possible.

CONTENTS

MAMMALS

BIRDS

GALLERY

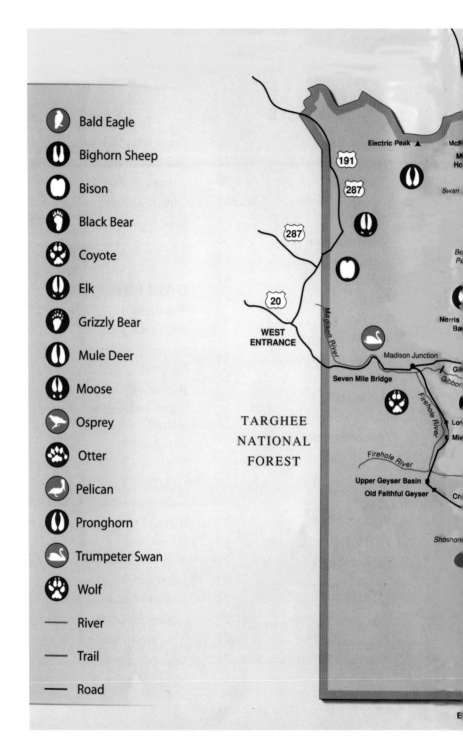

Bald Eagle

Bighorn Sheep

Bison

Black Bear

Coyote

Elk

Grizzly Bear

Mule Deer

Moose

Osprey

Otter

Pelican

Pronghorn

Trumpeter Swan

Wolf

— River

— Trail

— Road

TARGHEE
NATIONAL
FOREST

Electric Peak ▲

191

287

287

20

WEST
ENTRANCE

Madison River

Swan

Norris
Ba

Madison Junction

Seven Mile Bridge

Gibbon

Firehole River

Firehole River

Upper Geyser Basin
Old Faithful Geyser

Shoshone

Yellowstone National Park

GALLATIN NATIONAL FOREST

NORTH
TRANCE
iner

NORTHEAST
ENTRANCE

212

N

Yellowstone River

Floating Island Lake

Roosevelt
Tower Junction

liff

Soda Butte Creek

Lamar River

Tower Falls

Grand Canyon of Yellowstone

Mount Washburn

Dunraven Pass

Canyon
Village

rris
tion

Lower Falls

Upper Falls

SHOSHONE
NATIONAL FOREST

Lake Village

Fishing Bridge

Bridge Bay

EAST
ENTRANCE

14

16

20

Yellowstone Lake

Sylvan Pass

st Thumb

Grant Village

Yellowstone River

Snake River

20

191

BRIDGER-TETON

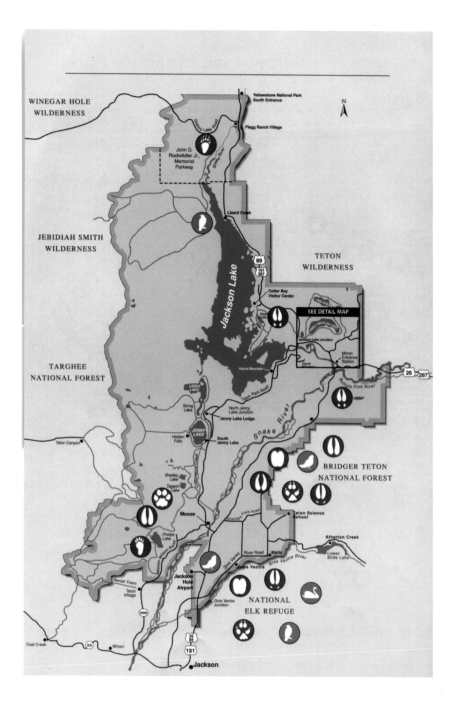

WINEGAR HOLE
WILDERNESS

Yellowstone National Park
South Entrance

Flagg Ranch Village

John D.
Rockefeller Jr.
Memorial
Parkway

Lizard Creek

JEBIDIAH SMITH
WILDERNESS

Jackson Lake

89
191
287

TETON
WILDERNESS

Colter Bay
Visitor Center

SEE DETAIL MAP

Jackson Lake Junction

Moran
Entrance
Station

26
287

Signal Mountain

Buffalo Fork River

TARGHEE
NATIONAL FOREST

LEIGH
LAKE

Teton Park Road

String
Lake

North Jenny
Lake Junction

Jenny Lake Lodge

Snake River

Teton Canyon

Hidden
Falls

JENNY
LAKE

South
Jenny Lake

BRIDGER TETON
NATIONAL FOREST

Bradley
Lake

Taggart
Lake

Moose

Teton Science
School

Phelps
Lake

Antelope Flats Road

Atherton Creek

River Road

Kelly

Lower
Slide Lake

Gros Ventre

Gros Ventre River

Aerial Tram

Teton
Village

Jackson
Hole
Airport

Gros Ventre
Junction

NATIONAL
ELK REFUGE

390

Coal Creek

22

Wilson

26
89
191

191

Jackson

Grand Teton National Park

Bald Eagle		Moose	
Birds of Prey		Pelican	
Bison		Pronghorn	
Black Bear		Sage Grouse	
Coyote		Trumpeter Swan	
Elk		Wading Birds	
Golden Eagle		—— River	
Grizzly Bear		—— Trail	
Mountain Lion		—— Road	
Mule Deer			

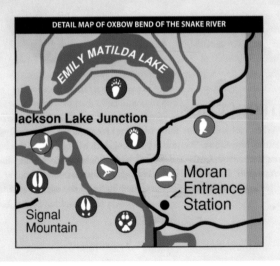

DETAIL MAP OF OXBOW BEND OF THE SNAKE RIVER

EMILY MATILDA LAKE

Jackson Lake Junction

Moran Entrance Station

Signal Mountain

INTRODUCTION

When global travelers think of embarking on a wildlife safari with their cameras, they picture the grand plains of Africa. They carry the images of nomadic elephant herds and stampeding wildebeests, predatory lions, and antelope prey. They envision a wild kingdom without parallel.

But in the rugged heart of the United States, at the edge of a vast, ancient volcanic crater, another panorama—this one straddling the northern Rocky Mountains—is equally renowned for its wild landscapes. Set aside in 1872, Yellowstone is not only America's first and oldest national park, it has become the icon of protected areas worldwide.

Together with Grand Teton National Park, it forms the biological heart of the greater Yellowstone ecosystem. Yellowstone's sheer geographical dimension confirms that this is no drive-through zoo. Sprawling across 3,400 square miles, it is larger than the combined states of Rhode Island and Delaware. Dotted with 10,000 geysers, hot springs, and boiling rivers, it has more rare geothermal phenomena than are encompassed on the rest of the planet. Graced by senescent pine forests, thundering waterfalls, jeweled blue lakes, and peaceful, verdant valleys, Yellowstone evokes the same surreal wonderment today that it did for the first visitors ten millennia ago.

The pretty scenery, however, is merely a backdrop to one of the most spectacular gatherings of wildlife anywhere on Earth. During the mid 1990s, with the successful reintroduction of gray wolves, Yellowstone achieved a kind of ecological completeness that other parks in the lower 48 states cannot match.

Today, Yellowstone is sanctuary to all of the large mammals that were here at the end of the Pleistocene epoch. Consider just a few of the species on Yellowstone's wildlife-watching checklist: grizzly bears and black bears, gray wolves, mountain lions, coyotes, bison, elk, pronghorn, bighorn sheep, moose, mule deer, trumpeter swans, bald eagles, peregrine falcons, river otter, and a famous namesake fish, the Yellowstone cutthroat trout.

As "the Serengeti of North America," Yellowstone's wildlife kingdom presents us with a magnificent paradox—resplendent, untamed populations of animals visually accessible from the roadside. This alone has made Yellowstone and its sister park, Grand Teton, a favorite destination for international wildlife photographers, but you needn't be a professional naturalist to appreciate these parks' novel place in the modern world.

Still, you have a question: "Where do I begin?" Roughly a century ago, John Muir, a pillar in the fledgling American conservation movement, came to Yellowstone via a mode of transportation that today seems archaic. Touring the national park in a horse-drawn carriage, Muir experienced the landscape differently than do the millions of tourists who pass through Yellowstone in our time.

His journey was slow and bumpy, but his wildlife watching was magnificent. Muir observed the wild denizens of Yellowstone because he took his time. Consider this book a valuable companion for planning your journey.

It will be more successful if you remember four basic tenets:

First, learn to identify the habitat, because it provides clues about which animals are likely to be present.

Second, be cognizant of the time of day, and recognize that the best times for seeing wildlife are at dawn and dusk.

Third, use this book to help you find the species you're looking for by referring to the suggested routes and tips.

Fourth, when you arrive at a choice location, relax and tune up your senses. Like Muir, be patient, listen, and wait.

A Brief Note About Grand Teton

Grand Teton National Park was established in 1929 and over the following two decades the boundaries of the park grew to encompass 484 square miles. Most visitors do not come to Grand Teton for the wildlife viewing. With bear-toothed summits as spectacular as the Teton Range, it is difficult, in fact, to pull one's eyes away from the sky-scraping peaks back down to earth. Yet between the lush riparian corridor of the Snake River, the jeweled lakes at the foot of the Tetons, and the carpet of sagebrush spilling east toward the Gros Ventre mountains, Grand Teton is a national park with exceptional opportunities for the field naturalist.

Six Routes Full of Wildlife

Whether you can stay a week or spend just a day, we suggest the following routes to maximize your wildlife viewing. They are the favorite haunts of professional wildlife photographers.

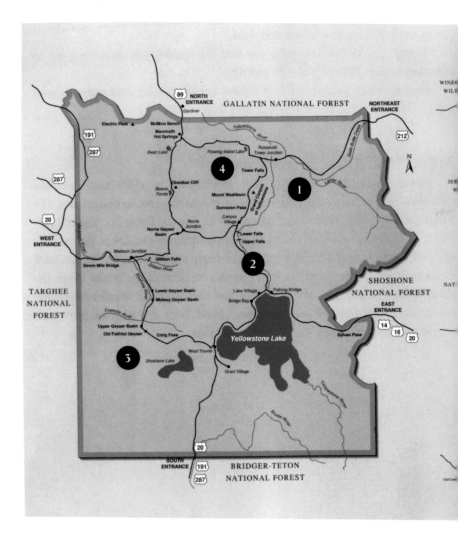

1. THE LAMAR VALLEY

The northern grasslands of Yellowstone, which roll across the Blacktail Plateau into the Lamar Valley, have been called "the Serengeti Plain of North America." From Roosevelt Junction to the northeast park entrance, the road travels through a picturesque dell that affords excellent opportunities for viewing wolves, grizzly bears, coyotes, elk, bison, bighorn sheep, badgers, raptors, and numerous small mammals and songbirds.

2. HAYDEN VALLEY TO YELLOWSTONE LAKE

Bisected by the Yellowstone River, Hayden Valley is another premier area for wildlife viewing in Yellowstone. Terrestrial animals and waterfowl abound. Come here to see bison, grizzly bears, wolves, American white pelicans, coyotes, occasional trumpeter swans, mule deer, harlequin ducks, river otters, bald eagles, and many other species.

3. UPPER GEYSER BASIN near OLD FAITHFUL TO THE MADISON RIVER

Set in a backdrop of geysers, hot springs, and fumeroles (thermal vents spewing steam), this section of the park is aesthetically surreal. Walking through the mist are elk and bison, occasional grizzly bears, wolves, and coyotes. Along the Madison and Firehole rivers, you may see river otters, trumpeter swans, bald eagles, great blue herons, and sandhill cranes.

4. OBSIDIAN CLIFF TO BLACKTAIL PLATEAU

This drive, which begins south of Mammoth Hot Springs and ends at Roosevelt Junction, offers opportunities for seeing mule deer, bison, black bears, grizzlies, wolves, trumpeter swans. coyotes, moose, badgers, elk, and pronghorn.

5. THE OXBOW BEND OF THE SNAKE RIVER

In Grand Teton, the premier wildlife-watching venue is Oxbow Bend along the Snake River west of Moran. Here, you can see bald eagles, moose, elk, river otter, beaver, a variety of wading birds and songbirds, and occasionally black bears and coyotes, among other species.

6. THE NATIONAL ELK REFUGE

While not officially part of Grand Teton National Park, the 24,700-acre National Elk Refuge, located between the national park and the town of Jackson, hosts a remarkable gathering of elk during the winter. The rest of the year you may also see bison, coyotes, wolves, bears, badgers, trumpeter swans, white pelicans, sandhill cranes, golden eagles, and other raptors.

A Wildlife Watcher's Code of Conduct

Next to loss of habitat, nothing is more destructive to native wildlife than humans who refuse to leave animals alone in their natural element. When you enter Yellowstone, you are accepting personal responsibility for your own behavior and that means acknowledging these ethical considerations that pertain to wildlife watching:

If an animal must change its behavior due to your presence, you're probably too close. If you feel compelled to get a closer glimpse of a wild creature along the roadside, enlist the help of binoculars, a spotting scope, or a longer camera lens. Remember, the chances of a harmful encounter increase exponentially as you invade an animal's space. Keeping your distance takes on greater importance during the winter months, when animals are strained by the bitter cold and lack of food. For example, the elk and bison you see along the roadside in winter are living off limited fat reserves that will help them survive until spring. By approaching a roadside animal and forcing it to flee, you may be hastening the animal's death.

Never feed wildlife. Not only is it unethical, but in Yellowstone it is punishable by a fine. Unlike animals in a zoo, Yellowstone's wild inhabitants are dependent on natural food for survival. Tossing your dinner

scraps in the direction of an animal is a gesture that could produce serious and deadly consequences. Animals that become habituated to human foods may someday attack an unsuspecting visitor whom they view as a food source, or they may starve when all the visitors have gone home. Every year, animals that become habituated to human food must either be killed or removed from the ecosystem.

Pets, particularly barking dogs, are a liability. They can affect wildlife watching because their presence is likely to frighten or attract the animals you're trying to spot and some pets will even chase wildlife. It is poor manners to let your pet out of the car where other people are

watching wildlife. In Yellowstone, every pet must be under the owner's control and on a leash at all times.

Never approach bird nests because human scent encourages abandonment of the nest by adult birds and can lead to predation by coyotes and other predators. Always afford animals with babies a wide berth and recognize that mothers with offspring will not hesitate to attack humans who are perceived as a threat.

Invariably during your visit to Yellowstone and Grand Teton, you may come upon a "bear jam," an "elk jam," a "wolf jam," or a "bison jam," colloquial terms which refer to backed-up traffic caused by the presence of an animal in close proximity to the road. Indeed, the prospect of seeing a grizzly bear or wolf or bull elk is exciting, but sometimes motorists abandon common sense. When you come upon a scene of backed-up traffic caused by an animal, try to find a designated turnout to park your car to help prevent damage to roadside vegetation. If that is not possible, pull your car over to the side as safely as possible and be mindful of steep inclines sloping away from the road. Always reduce your speed when approaching "animal jams," watching out for people scampering into the road as well as animals.

Most animals identified in this book might be viewed at any hour of the day from the roadside. But remember, the most productive periods for wildlife watchers are the hours around dawn and dusk. At high noon, your prospects of seeing secretive animals are poorest, while early morning and the few hours prior to sunset usually yield the best results.

Travelers in the parks may not realize that their vehicle can provide an effective blind (hide) for wildlife watching. Most species have become accustomed to the steady flow of human vehicles on the highway and exhibit more tolerance for a car than the two-legged animals inside of them. For watching large and sometimes dangerous animals like bears, bison, and moose, vehicles also provide you with safety.

Wildlife Encounters and Checklist

COMMON: On any given day, you should encounter one or more of this species.

OCCASIONAL: By simply driving through the park without any information, you may see the species on chance encounters. However, by using the tips and suggested locations in this book, you have a good chance of seeing the animal.

RARE: While these animals have been seen in Yellowstone and Grand Teton, they are viewed so rarely that it's impossible to predict when or where you might observe them.

■ Common ◪ Occasional □ Rare

MAMMALS

Grizzly Bear	◪	Wolverine	□
Black Bear	◪	Badger	◪
Bison (Buffalo)	■	River Otter	◪
Moose	◪	Pine Marten	◪
Elk (Wapiti)	■	Fisher	□
Mule Deer	■	Mink	◪
White-tailed Deer	□	Weasel	◪
Bighorn Sheep	◪	Beaver	◪
Mountain Goat	□	Muskrat	◪
Pronghorn (Antelope)	■	Snowshoe Hare	◪
Gray Wolf	◪	Uinta Ground Squirrel	■
Coyote	◪	Red Squirrel	■
Red Fox	□	Marmot	■
Mountain Lion	□	Pika	■
Bobcat	□	Least Chipmunk	■
Lynx	□	Yellow-pine Chipmunk	■
Porcupine	◪		

BIRDS

Bald Eagle	◪	Sandhill Crane	◪
Golden Eagle	◪	Whooping Crane	□
Osprey	■	Canada Goose	■
Peregrine Falcon	□	Harlequin Duck	□
Red-tailed Hawk	■	Common Raven	■
Great Gray Owl	◪	Ruffed Grouse	◪
American White Pelican	◪	Blue Grouse	◪
Trumpeter Swan	◪	Sage Grouse	◪
Great Blue Heron	◪		

MAMMALS

GRIZZLY BEAR

According to park rangers, no wildlife question is asked more frequently than "Where are the grizzly bears and wolves?" The second most common question is "How many people are attacked and killed by bears in Yellowstone each year?"

Statistics show that during Yellowstone's first hundred years (1872 to 1972), fewer than a dozen people were fatally mauled by bears, though scores of visitors were injured when they ventured too close to bruins that wanted to be left alone.

The biggest mistake made by visitors is believing that bears are tame. Accident reports in both Yellowstone and Grand Teton prove otherwise.

Feeding bears is not only dangerous but it encourages these animals to forsake natural food for human handouts, a habit that has resulted in human injury and the forced destruction of many bears. Feeding them even once trains them to seek human foods. From 1931 to 1969, an average of 46 people were injured annually by bears in Yellowstone, and an average of 24 bears were killed each year.

This said, it is impossible not to enjoy an endless fascination with these large mammals. Certainly in the lower 48 states, no wild animal is more daunting than a grizzly. When frontier taxonomists first encountered grizzlies in the nineteenth century, the bears' brawny size and dangerous demeanor inspired them to bestow the scientific name, *Ursus arctos horribilis,* Latin for "horrible bear."

Yet today, few people fortunate enough

to safely watch Yellowstone grizzlies in the wild are likely to draw the same conclusion. Large, nomadic, and aggressive, the grizzly embodies the spirit of primeval wilderness, and its mere presence is enough to make our hearts beat faster.

Less than 200 years ago, there were perhaps 100,000 grizzlies inhabiting North America, but with human settlement of the West, grizzlies today occupy less than one percent of their original habitat in the lower 48 states.

Viable numbers of these great bruins persist in just two ecosystems south of Canada—the greater Yellowstone ecosystem, which includes both Yellowstone and Grand Teton national parks

and a few surrounding national forests; and the Crown of the Continent ecosystem, which includes Glacier National Park and the adjoining Bob Marshall-Scapegoat wilderness areas.

In 1975, the Yellowstone grizzly was formally listed as a "threatened" species under the Endangered Species Act. Biologists studying the bear knew that unless drastic action was taken to safeguard bear habitat and reduce the number of bruin deaths caused by clashes with humans, the species would soon become regionally extinct.

Thanks to foresighted bear management, aimed at reducing the number of human-bear conflicts by getting bears to focus on natural food, the Yellowstone grizzly population has rebounded from a population crash that occurred in the early 1980s.

The short-term prognosis for grizzlies is positive. In fact, park visitors stand as good a chance of seeing grizzlies today as they did in the halcyon days of the 1950s when begging bruins habituated to human foods were common along the roadsides.

Grizzlies often inhabit home ranges that cover hundreds of square miles, which speaks to their need for undisturbed wild country. Weighing as much as 600 pounds, individual bears can outsprint a horse over short distances and mother bears are notoriously temperamental when it comes to protecting their cubs.

Grizzly bears are omnivores, meaning they eat both meat and plants. Knowing their dietary habits helps inform the wildlife watcher on where to find them at certain times of the year. In the spring, for instance, bears are often viewed at lower elevations scavenging on the carcasses of winter-killed bison and elk. During the summer, they often are sighted while foraging for berries, elk calves, plants, and spawning trout in the streams surrounding Yellowstone Lake. As autumn approaches, bears can be observed in the high country filling their bellies with whitebark pine nuts, army cutworm moths, and plant roots.

Wildlife watchers should look for certain physical characteristics to help distinguish grizzlies from black bears. Two features associated with grizzlies are their dish-shaped faces (as opposed to more conical shapes on black bears) and a muscular shoulder hump. The hue of a grizzly's coat, like that of a black bear, may range from tawny cinnamon to light brown or even black. Some grizzlies are flecked with recognizable "silver tips," creating a "grizzled" look that is partially responsible for the bear's common name.

During the long winter months in Yellowstone, grizzlies sleep in underground dens, where females give birth to cubs. Their slumbering dormancy enables bears to live off fat deposits acquired during the warm-weather months. Female bears have a unique adaptation when it comes to pregnancy. While breeding between boars (males) and sows (females) occurs in early summer, a female is able to delay development of the fetus for many weeks, until she has reached the den.

Beginning usually in December, the fertilized eggs grow in the mother's womb over a gestation period of 45 to 60 days. Although a sow may show no sign of pregnancy in late autumn, she emerges in the spring with a brood of one to three cubs. Generally, bears leave their dens in March with solitary males emerging first.

Along the trail or near some roadside locations mentioned below, you may find evidence that a grizzly traveled through the area prior to your arrival. Bear scat (feces) resembles the human variety and provides hints of what the animals are eating. Among other indicators of grizzly presence are paw prints. All members of the ursid (bear) family are plantigrade, meaning that they walk on the flat of their feet instead of walking on their toes. Given their weight, grizzlies may leave behind an indented print in the mud or snow. Like humans, grizzlies have five toes, though the biggest toe lies on the outside of the foot, not on the inside.

Seeing a grizzly requires patience and a keen eye. Successful nature photographers report that the twilight hours of early morning and late afternoon offer the best viewing opportunities. During these times, grizzlies move out of forests into open meadows. Approximately one of every five bears in Yellowstone has been equipped with a research collar that can be tracked using radio telemetry or global positioning systems. If you see a grizzly, report the sighting to a ranger. The information may be useful to biologists who are tracking the movements of bears around the park. When bears are close and along the roadside, do not leave the safety of your car.

Where To Find Grizzly Bears

In Yellowstone, look along Dunraven Pass between Canyon Village and the Tower-Roosevelt area. Some of the most frequent sightings of grizzlies are made just off the northern slope of 8,850-foot Dunraven

Pass, north of the Chittenden Road turnoff and along the turnouts overlooking the Antelope Creek drainage. Antelope Creek is a bear management area closed off to hikers but it is visually accessible from the roadside, particularly with a high-powered spotting scope or long camera lens. Most grizzly sightings are reported here between late May and June, when the road opens, through mid-October.

In the Lamar Valley bears frequent the area between Roosevelt Junction and the northeast park entrance just west of Cooke City. Near the east entrance of Yellowstone, bears have been viewed from spring to late fall in the vicinity of the Shoshone River east of Pahaska Tepee, just outside the park border on the road to Cody. In recent years, grizzlies have often been seen from the road between Norris and Mammoth, wandering the wooded hills between Roaring Mountain and Obsidian Cliff.

Bears are also viewed from the northern outlet of Yellowstone Lake near Fishing Bridge northward into the Hayden Valley. In late spring, dozens of grizzlies converge upon Yellowstone Lake tributaries to feast upon spawning cutthroat trout. Hiking trails leading to these streams are closed to minimize conflict between bears and people. However, bears are routinely sighted along the roadside, especially in Hayden Valley. Once you arrive in the valley's open expanse, watch for overlooks on the east side of the highway and try to locate bears wandering across the undulating meadows as far back as the treeline. Dawn and dusk are the best times of day.

Another good viewing area is the southwestern shore of Yellowstone Lake, between West Thumb and Grant Village. Along the shore of Yellowstone Lake from Mary Bay to Lake Butte Overlook, bears are sometimes seen in the morning and evening. Many grizzlies are spotted near the lake in late spring and early summer as bears converge upon tributary streams where cutthroat trout spawn.

In Grand Teton, grizzlies have just begun to exert a presence as the greater Yellowstone grizzly population expands its range. The best chance of spotting a grizzly in Grand Teton is in the northern sections of the park, along the remote northern shores of Jackson Lake, in the river bottoms of the Snake River, on the highway connecting the town of Moran with Dubois over Togwotee Pass, and along the John D. Rockefeller Memorial Parkway leading to Yellowstone's south entrance station.

BLACK BEAR

In Yellowstone, some visitors look upon black bears as "the little brothers of the grizzly." Together, black bears and grizzlies have given the park its global reputation as a bear preserve.

The black bear's scientific and Latin name, *Ursus americanus*, means "American bear." Indeed, endemic black bears are the most widely distributed bruins in North America, found from the forests of Canada to the bogs of the southeastern United States.

More numerous than grizzlies, black bears seem to be visually rarer than their larger cousins and there is some dispute over the size of Yellowstone's black bear population. According to loose estimates, roughly 650 black bears inhabit the park. Surprisingly little is known about the behavior and demography of Yellowstone black bears because most field studies and federal research dollars to date have focused on grizzlies.

Compared to grizzlies, black bears are generally more docile, though males (boars) and females (sows) have been known to attack humans who accidentally stumble upon a cache of food or wander too close to cubs.

The primary misconception about black bears is that all of them are black. Depending upon genes of their parents, the fur coloring of individual bears can be reddish tan, blond, chocolate brown, or jet-black. Brown-colored black bears are often mistaken for small grizzlies. The size of black bears helps distinguish between the two species. Adult males weigh between 200 and 400 pounds while sows weigh between 150 and 400 pounds. Adult grizzlies are far bigger in physical stature. Of course, there are other differences that should be helpful in identification.

A black bear's rump is higher than its shoulder and black bears have a "Roman nose" instead of the grizzly's dish-shaped face. Scat is tube-shaped and similar in appearance to both grizzly scat and the feces of humans.

Tracks reflect the black bear's classification as a plantigrade, or flat-footed walker. The front and rear paw prints look almost like a human's, with five toes and paws leaving impressions that are shallower in front and deeper in back.

Having adapted to forests over thousands of years, black bears are adept at climbing trees. These escape routes from danger often are used by frightened cubs. Grizzlies, encumbered by long claws, are not as skilled at ascending Yellowstone's tall and skinny conifers.

Less reliant on brute strength or a dominating appearance, black bears prey less often upon large game animals, instead employing superb scavenging techniques. During the seven or eight months prior to winter denning, they consume a diverse plant and meat diet ranging from berries and plant tubers to small rodents, animal carcasses, and elk calves when available.

The black bear's roving nature often brings these bruins into open meadows at night and early morning. By happy coincidence, wildlife watchers often are treated to black bear sightings from the road. The historic forest fires of 1988 affected a large section of bear terrain along park roads and it is conceivable that bear sightings may increase in the burned drainages now experiencing spikes in the amount of available plants and small mammals. Scientists still are not clear about how habitat for black bears and grizzlies overlaps. Both species are vulnerable to poachers as the Asian folk medicine market for bear gall bladders, paws, claws, and other bruin body parts thrives. Fortunately, because of the geographical isolation of Yellowstone's backcountry and diligent ranger patrols, black bears here are less of a target for poachers than in other parts of the country.

Where To Find Black Bears

In Yellowstone, be attentive as you cross the Blacktail Plateau between Mammoth Hot Springs and Tower-Roosevelt junction, and scan the meadows between Tower and Antelope Creek south of Tower Falls.

The stretch of highway between Undine Falls and Floating Island Lake south and east of Mammoth should be considered a prime area for possible black bear sightings, as should the river flood plain of the Gardner River.

In Grand Teton, black bear sightings along the interior road located between the lakes at the foot of the Tetons and the Snake River to the east flourished during the 1990s. In addition, several black bears had to be relocated to other areas after attacking humans along the Snake River. Be alert and remember that keeping a clean camp is the best defense against encountering an aggressive bear.

Perhaps the best strategy for finding a bear is to inquire at park visitor centers. If you spot a bear on the road, report it to park officials because the information can help biologists in planning their wildlife management strategies.

GRAY WOLF

The pack is back! With primordial howls again filling the mountain valleys of Yellowstone, the return of the gray wolf is, without question, one of the great success stories in modern wildlife conservation.

Wolves were essentially extinct in the Yellowstone region until the mid-1990s, the victims of misguided predator control campaigns waged earlier in the twentieth century. By the late 1920s, wolves had been shot, trapped, and poisoned out of existence. Disappearing with them went an important wild component of the ecosystem.

The gray wolf *(Canis lupus)* is the largest of North America's wild canid predators and is identical to the wolves inhabiting Alaska, Canada, and the upper Midwest of the United States. Gray wolves weigh between 50 and 130 pounds and mother wolves use dens to bear and raise pups, but the animals do not hibernate in winter. In fact, during the coldest months wolves are active and effective hunters.

Although myths and fairy tales abound with accounts of "evil" wolves, in the U.S. there has never been a documented case in which a healthy, wild wolf has killed a person. Generally, wolves prefer to keep their distance from humans and are highly secretive.

Much can be said about how wolves help "regulate" other wildlife populations, but, in fact, these mammalian carnivores are actually part of a larger dynamic involving predators and prey that still is not fully understood. A delight to wildlife watchers is that in Yellowstone they will have a front-row seat to watch this grand experiment for generations to come.

Begun with two shipments of Canadian wolves in the mid 1990s, Yellowstone's wolf population surpassed 100 individual lobos in 1998 and the number continues to grow. Three primary factors have enabled wolves to flourish: (1) Abundant natural prey. Large numbers of elk, which migrate in and out of the park seasonally, provide a continuous year-round food source; (2) Habitat. Between Yellowstone and the surrounding national forests, wolves have large, untrammeled expanses of public lands on which to roam and establish home ranges and territories; (3) Successful breeding and production of pups. Wolf packs are led by dominant alpha males and alpha females, which generally are the only animals to breed in a given pack. Wolves breed in the winter and give birth to pups in the spring.

Once packs are established, younger pack members occasionally

leave the family unit and start their own clan. Biologists say the number of wolf packs in the Greater Yellowstone region is a function of the natural prey and the quality of the habitat.

Despite fierce resistance from the regional livestock industry and legal attempts to block wolf reintroduction, biologists say the hysteria surrounding the alleged threat of wolves to the livelihoods of farmers and ranchers has been largely unfounded. Not only are wolves killing less livestock in areas outside the park than expected, but the conservation organization, Defenders of Wildlife, has created a special fund that compensates ranchers for any cattle or sheep lost to wolf predation.

Still another fear, also unfounded, came from some sportsmen's groups that asserted that wolves would decimate populations of game animals, namely, elk, deer, moose, and bighorn sheep. While the presence of wolves certainly has changed the behavior of game animals, those prey species continue to thrive.

Wolves are second only to grizzly bears in popularity and mystique. Each year, tens of thousands of visitors are able to watch wolves because the open landscape lends itself to good observation.

Where To Find Wolves

During the winter months wolves are commonly seen in the Lamar Valley. Many of the wolves are dark colored and thus show up well against the snow. Wolves are also seen frequently in the Blacktail Lakes area during the winter months. Wherever you are, watch for large groups of people with tripods and spotting scopes! It's a sure sign that wolves (or bears in the warmer months) are in the area.

As the number of packs has increased, new wolf territories have been staked out across the Hayden Valley and the geyser basins around Old Faithful. While sightings of wolves in these areas are erratic, it is not uncommon to hear wolf howls in the evening hours and just before sunrise.

In Grand Teton, wolf packs have slowly begun colonizing northern reaches of the park. Since wolf pack activity is tied to the availability of elk and other prey species, biologists say it is inevitable that wolves will follow migratory wapiti to the National Elk Refuge, located between the northern city limits of Jackson and Grand Teton National Park. Every winter, thousands of elk gather on the refuge to eat supplemental forage and then disperse during the spring and summer months in the national parks and surrounding national forests. Eventually the National Elk Refuge may well provide one of the best opportunities to observe wild wolves and prey in the world.

COYOTE

Known as "the trickster" in Native American mythology, the coyote (*Canis latrans*) is one of the most adaptive carnivores in the world. Once a species that existed almost exclusively west of the Mississippi River, the coyote dramatically expanded its range in the twentieth century and is now found from the Alaskan tundra to the subtropical climes of Florida, in every U.S. state except Hawaii.

Intelligent and social animals, coyotes grow as large as a medium-sized dog. Their fur color varies according to habitat and parental genetics, though in Yellowstone the majority of adults have gray-brown coats with a whitish underbelly, bushy tail, and reddish hair on the front and back legs. On average, coyotes weigh between 30 and 40 pounds, about half as much as a wolf. Their noses, heads, legs, and feet are less prominent. Wolves have broader muzzles, massive heads, long legs, and huge feet.

During the sixty-year absence of the gray wolf—the coyote's natural enemy—the coyote population in Yellowstone swelled. In the park's northern valleys alone, recent studies showed a coyote population of 500 individuals encompassed by sixty distinct packs. The same studies also indicated that coyotes had claimed the former wolf niche and prospered on an abundance of natural food sources, from insects and berries to small rodents, wild birds, and even young elk. As such, the coyote is the ultimate opportunist when it comes to scavenging and can get by on whatever the landscape provides. With the return of wolves, coyote numbers in Yellowstone have decreased dramatically.

The coyote is a rover like the African jackal, seemingly always on the move. It's normal for small groups of coyotes to amble dozens of miles during a night of hunting. When in pursuit of prey, they can spring at speeds of 35 to 40 miles per hour. Like wolves, coyotes are pack animals that work together to bring down young deer, pronghorn, or elk calves.

A fascinating behavior trait, observed in Yellowstone, is that a coyote will join badgers in hunting. As the badger plows through the den of a ground squirrel, the coyote will wait near the rodent's escape hatch.

There are several clues signifying coyote presence. First, listen for yips and howls, the famous singing sounds associated with the species. Scan the ground for coyote tracks, which can be 3 to 5 inches across.

Although coyotes are night hunters in many areas, they do not fear humans in Yellowstone so they are active at all hours. The management of coyotes in Yellowstone is typical for a national park, which does not normally allow shooting of animals, but for the West it is unusual. Outside Yellowstone's boundaries, coyotes are regarded as vermin by cattle and sheep ranchers, who shoot them at will.

Habituation to human food is regarded as a great threat to coyotes, for animals that have been fed will aggressively approach people. Some encounters have been dangerous. For obvious reasons, you should never feed coyotes. The table scraps you leave behind could become a death sentence for a coyote or could result in human injury.

Where To Find Coyotes

Look for them year-round in the Lamar Valley along the roadsides. Because of wolves, coyotes have been forced to exist in closer proximity to humans where wolves do not venture.

Coyotes are also viewed along the shores of Yellowstone Lake, in the Hayden Valley, the geyser basins around Norris and Old Faithful, and the Blacktail Plateau.

In Grand Teton, coyotes are ubiquitous. They often are spotted in the eastern sections of the park along the Gros Ventre River Road to the town of Kelly; along the inner park road (Teton Park Road) in the sagebrush meadows at the foot of the Tetons, and throughout the National Elk Refuge.

RED FOX

The red fox (*Vulpes vulpes*) is the shyest wild canid in the Yellowstone region and seldom seen, when compared to wolves or coyotes. Although red foxes are abundant in the lower agricultural river valleys outside the park, the foxes of Yellowstone are far more discreet. Studies suggest that the higher elevations of Yellowstone and adjacent mountains may actually be home to an endemic species of fox that exists in isolation from other native red foxes and those introduced to the continent by Europeans.

Red foxes are common throughout most of North America, and the animal's "cunning" ability to outfox hunters and fur trappers is legendary. Night hunters that prowl the forest edges and meadows, these omnivores have smaller territories than coyotes but they will hunt across wide areas nonetheless.

Wildlife watchers shouldn't have a problem differentiating between red foxes and coyotes. An adult fox weighs about 15 pounds, perhaps half the weight of a small adult coyote. Foxes also have a

classic long, slender snout. Unlike wolves and coyotes, foxes rarely howl or sing as a form of gregariousness. What sets the fox apart, of course, is the color of its fur. As the name suggests, the typical red fox has orange-red fur. The fox has a spot of white on the tip of its fluffy black and red tail. The underside of its body, from neck to posterior, is covered by a creamy white fur, and its paws are dark or black. However, note that some "red" foxes may be all gray or reddish blond. As with black bears, red foxes take on hues other than the color for which they are primarily known.

The red fox generally subsists upon a variety of rodents but has other dietary staples such as grasshoppers and berries. In learning more about foxes, we begin to understand how predators interrelate. The reintroduction of wolves to Yellowstone may impart some long-term benefits for foxes by producing a lower coyote population, which is a fox competitor. Also, carcasses left behind by wolves might benefit foxes, too.

Never, under any circumstances, approach or attempt to feed a fox. The animal will bite if provoked and it can carry rabies. However, no Yellowstone canid—fox, coyote, or wolf—has tested positive for rabies since the park was founded in 1872.

Where To Find Red Foxes

The timid nature of foxes means they are less visible from the road than coyotes. Sightings are infrequent and often seasonal, with most occurring in winter, spring, or autumn around Canyon Village. In meadows that roll away from the Grand Canyon of the Yellowstone River, foxes are occasionally spotted from the roadside as they hunt at dusk and dawn. Red "mountain" foxes are also sighted occasionally along the slopes of Mount Washburn, which rise above Dunraven Pass, and in the northeastern corner of the park on the slopes of the Absaroka and Beartooth mountains above the towns of Silver Gate and Cooke City.

In Grand Teton, red foxes are sighted occasionally in the open meadowlands around park headquarters in Moose and along the Antelope Flats Road.

MOUNTAIN LION

Sleek, stealthy, powerful, feared—mountain lions are formidable predators known to humans by many names. Depending upon the region of the country, they might also take the moniker puma, cougar, or catamount.

Mountain lions are the largest members of the cat family native to North America and they are this continent's version of the African lion. Their scientific name, *Felis concolor*, means "cat of one color." Weighing between 75 and 200 pounds at adulthood, these tawny carnivores have no natural enemies except humans. Agile and fleet, a mature lion can leap nearly 20 feet in a single bound from waiting in ambush, which is a preferred hunting method.

Given Yellowstone's abundant prey diversity—elk, deer, bighorn sheep, pronghorn, and a range of smaller mammals and birds—the park and its adjacent rugged canyons provide exceptional cat habitat.

Mountain lions may roam 20 or more miles in a night. The fact that these wild cats are so seldom seen in the wild, however, makes them an enigma when it comes to wildlife watching. Your odds of seeing a mountain lion from the road are significantly poorer than, say, the odds of being struck by lightning while on a hike.

These elusive felids are predominantly night hunters. They usually occupy rocky sections of the backcountry and there is little reason for a mountain lion to venture near developed areas of the park unless they are coping with a bad year for natural. Rest

assured, never in Yellowstone's recorded history has there been a documented instance in which a mountain lion severely injured a person. In fact, few park rangers have even seen a mountain lion in the wild.

The lion's low profile among the other mighty predators can also be attributed to low numbers. During the first three decades of the twentieth century, federal hunters and trappers were hired to eradicate mountain lions and other predators that preyed upon popular park wildlife, such as deer and elk. The belief then was that by killing predators, large numbers of the other animals would exist indefinitely. But nature is far more complicated than that.

Fortunately, mountain lions were spared from complete eradication

and seemed to increase in number during the last few decades, but their low rate of reproduction and their need for a large range have kept the population at relatively reduced levels. Research has shown that about 20 lions occupy a study area measuring 320 square miles. Between 1960 and 1985, almost 300 reliable sightings of mountain lions were reported, most near winter ranges for elk. The number of mountain lion sightings in and around Yellowstone seems to be increasing.

Signs indicating mountain lion presence include copious scat ranging from dark spheres to pellets, often with traces of whatever the lion ingested, such as elk and deer hair or bones. Tracks are identical to those of a house cat but bigger, and wider than long. Mountain lions leave tracks in front paw/back paw pairs, where the prints are staggered and the front paw impressions overlap with those of the hind paws. They are usually between 3 and 5 inches across and show no claw marks because the claws are retracted when walking.

Although humans are their only natural enemy, these cats will tangle with coyotes in winters when food is in short supply. In more populated parts of the Rockies, lions have attacked children. The safest spot from which to view a mountain lion is the inside of your vehicle.

Where To Find Mountain Lions

In Yellowstone, it's improbable that you will see mountain lions from the roadside and even rarer to see them from the roadside in wide-open country without trees or side canyons into which they can escape. However, sightings of lions have been more frequent in the Lamar Valley and along the Yellowstone, Madison, and Gallatin river drainages. Specifically, sightings have been reported along the park highway east of Lamar Valley and the highway over Sylvan Pass outside the east entrance, and in the Tower-Roosevelt area.

In Grand Teton, mountain lion sightings have been reported along the Gros Ventre River and foothills and the rugged foothills of the Teton Range, especially in the vicinity of Phelps Lake.

LYNX

Victims of overharvest and loss of habitat, lynx in the lower 48 states have been in decline for several decades. While lynx (*Rufus canadensis*) inhabit Yellowstone, Grand Teton, and the surrounding national forests, little is known about their regional population size.

Similar in habits and range to their close cousin, the bobcat, lynx are famously dependent on local populations of snowshoe hare. When hare populations reach the peak of their cycle, lynx numbers also tend to be higher, and when hare numbers crash, lynx numbers decline.

Ecologists say the Yellowstone forest fires of 1988, by improving habitat for snowshoe hares, may help the status of the lynx in the decades ahead. A furtive prowler, the lynx is a wide-ranging hunter whose behavior parallels that of the mountain lion and the bobcat.

Like the bobcat, the lynx was eagerly sought by fur trappers, suffering as a result from some local extinctions. Today, it is a protected species in Wyoming and Idaho, but destruction of wilderness habitat continues to influence its presence outside Yellowstone and Grand Teton.

The lynx has a short tail that is ringed by alternating bands of color. The cat's long, silky coat is gray-buffed, sometimes augmented by blotches of brown on its belly. There is also a tuft of distinguishing striped fur under the lynx's chin but the classic marking is the black tuft rising above its ears.

Compared to the bobcat, the lynx has wider paws that, like snowshoes, enable it to maneuver across a deep snowpack. The paws themselves are furry between the toes and closely resemble the impressions of a house cat. If you believe you have spotted a lynx, report it immediately to park officials. The information will help them develop management strategies for lynx conservation.

Where To Find Lynx

Within Yellowstone and Grand Teton, lynx inhabit essentially the same kind of terrain as bobcats but often at higher elevations. Spotting a lynx is unlikely but in recent years observations have been made in the northeast corner of Yellowstone, along Sylvan Pass between Fishing Bridge and the east entrance, over Craig Pass southeast of Old Faithful, and near Yellowstone's southern entrance.

In Grand Teton, lynx sightings have been made north of Moran and inside the John D. Rockefeller Memorial Parkway.

BOBCAT

Bobcats *(Felis rufus)* are known to exist in Yellowstone and Grand Teton but not in large numbers. Little scientific research has been conducted to produce precise population estimates.

Bobcats are so named for their knobby, bobbed tails. While the coat of a bobcat is conspicuous—ranging from tawny brown in warm months to grayish in winter—the distinguishing marks of this cat are the many leopard-like black spots that flank its sides and legs. The outer reaches of its underbelly are mottled, while the center of the belly is white or a creamy color. A bobcat's face has irregular black stripes and has a black ring that is broken by white on the underside.

Like lynx, bobcats roam the forests and meadows wherever there are sufficient congregations of prey—small mammals, rodents, and birds. In both parks, the relative scarcity of bobcats may simply be due to available habitat. Since bobcats prefer rocky, windblown or south-facing slopes at lower elevations, neither park is particularly conducive to high numbers of these felids.

Historically, bobcats were trapped heavily, which caused local extinctions. There still is a hunting season on bobcats in the surrounding states. The bobcat is native only to the lower 48 states and southern areas of Canada. It may be further limited to areas of little snowfall, where total accumulation is 20 inches or less.

Bobcats hunt by stalking their prey at night and early morning. Except for humans and occasional skirmishes with lions, coyotes, or wolves, the bobcat has few enemies. They, too, will inhabit vast home ranges. It is rare that wildlife watchers see bobcats from the roadside.

Where To Find Bobcats

Sightings of bobcats in both Yellowstone and Grand Teton are rare. In Yellowstone, sightings have occurred in the northeast corner of the park and over Sylvan Pass between Fishing Bridge and the east entrance. There have also been sightings just inside Yellowstone's south entrance, inside the John D. Rockefeller Memorial Parkway and the northern forested interior of Grand Teton. Any bobcat sighting should be reported to park officials.

BISON (BUFFALO)

Whether peppering the rolling knolls of Hayden Valley, lumbering through the ethereal mist of geysers, or kicking up dust on the northern grasslands, Yellowstone's bison (*Bison bison*) herds are important ecological touchstones. As descendants of free-ranging buffalo that somehow survived the notorious slaughter of the nineteenth century, these woolly behemoths provide a direct connection to America's aboriginal past. Bison were once the most prolific native bovine anywhere in the world. Across the Great Plains and mountainous foothills, they numbered 60 million strong, but by the time Yellowstone was set aside in 1872, wild bison faced imminent extinction as a species. Fortunately, a small band of animals found hidden sanctuary in Yellowstone free from poachers and market meat hunters. Only through vigilant protection has the Yellowstone bison been able to persist.

Until the 1950s, the National Park Service operated the "Buffalo

Ranch" in Yellowstone's Lamar Valley near Rose Creek (today home to the Yellowstone Institute), where bison were carefully husbanded like cattle and managed to ensure a sustainable population. But then in the 1960s, park policy shaped by foresighted ecologists sought to end the program, promoting the idea of a naturally regulated herd controlled only by predators and the winter elements.

The whole notion of natural regulation has been controversial. Supporters of the policy say that Yellowstone's bison are illustrative of how the park is actually part of a larger ecosystem. Yellowstone's grasslands alone are insufficient to sustain large nomadic wildlife herds, which leave the park's high country in the winter and move to lower elevations. Park bison, in fact, have been doing this for millennia.

But opponents of natural regulation, namely ranchers associated with the cattle industry, have tried to keep free-ranging bison contained, not only because bison are difficult to control but because some animals carry the disease, brucellosis. As a bacterium that causes infected domestic cows to abort their fetuses, brucellosis is viewed as a major threat to cattle herds, but the actual risk of passing the disease from bison to cattle is a source of much dispute. Nonetheless, several thousand bison have been killed or sent to slaughterhouses because the cattle industry would like to keep Yellowstone's bison inside the park boundary.

Yellowstone bison are most active in the cool of morning and evening. Docile and seemingly oblivious to activity around them, bison exude a calm demeanor, sometimes misinterpreted by humans as an open invitation to approach. As the flyers distributed at park entrance stations warn, these 2,000-pound animals may seem tame but they are not.

It may be surprising to know that the number of park visitors that have been gored by bison since 1980 is three times the total number of humans attacked by both grizzly and black bears. Distance should be afforded bison, especially lone bulls that have sought seclusion or cows with young calves.

Where To Find Bison

The natural panorama of Hayden Valley in the center of Yellowstone is like a window into the past. Hundreds of bison can usually be photographed on a summer or autumn day, many near the roadside. Young bulls may be sparring, or adults may be seeking relief from the

summer heat by bathing in streams dissecting the valley floor.

The northern shore of Yellowstone Lake in the vicinities of both Fishing Bridge and the Lake Development provide excellent bison watching opportunities.

The upper and lower geyser basins stretching north from Old Faithful along the Firehole River give the photographer a spectacular backdrop in early morning and evening light.

In Grand Teton, a resident bison herd of a few hundred animals disperses across the meadowlands stretching from the town of Kelly on the east to the lakes northwest of park headquarters at Moose. During the winter, bison also congregate on the National Elk Refuge.

MOOSE

Moose are highly visible in both Yellowstone and Grand Teton. As the largest members of the deer family, the moose (*Alces alces*) is a long-lived, ravenous plant eater that seems charmingly oversized.

Next to bison, moose are the largest animals encountered in both parks. You will find them in slow-moving streams and creeks, in the riparian areas of rivers, and the backwater areas of lakes where they seek out aquatic plants. During the winter, they browse on the woody stems of shrubs and peel away tree bark.

Healthy bulls (males) and cows (females) can live into their twenties, reach staggering weights of 1,000 pounds or more, and achieve shoulder heights topping 7 feet. Blending in with their surroundings, moose are primitive in appearance but relative newcomers to Yellowstone. Biologists believe they immigrated into Yellowstone as late as the 1870s from the environs of Grand Teton and beyond, reaching the northern grasslands by about 1913. Today, a few hundred moose inhabit northern sections of Yellowstone and many more are found elsewhere in the park. Grand Teton's moose population, which proportionately is larger than Yellowstone's, also numbers several hundred and does not include several hundred others scattered around other parts of Jackson Hole and the Bridger-Teton National Forest.

Both bulls and cows are covered with a coat of dark brown hair that appears almost black when wet. Their hind legs show a white gleam at times. While the imposing palmate antlers are a trademark of bulls, both sexes share other pronounced physical features. The elongated snout, bulbous nose, and pendulous dewlap or "bell" under the throat distinguish them from other ungulates (hooved animals) in the ecosystem. Except during mating, bulls tend to be solitary, while cows stand guard over their calves (often twins) until the offspring are about a year old.

Where To Find Moose

In Yellowstone, the most popular place for moose viewing among wildlife photographers is Willow Park, a haven for moose located between Mammoth Hot Springs and Norris Junction.

During the spring, summer, and autumn months, you may see moose near Bridge Bay, Lake Village, and the Fishing Bridge developments. Another prime location is Phantom Lake northwest of Tower-Roosevelt, and roadside areas near the east and northeastern entrances to the park. Hikers in the Canyon Village and Lake areas frequently encounter cow moose with calves.

In Grand Teton, which offers moose viewing opportunities that surpass Yellowstone's, stake out the wildlife viewing turnouts near the Oxbow Bend of the Snake River west of Moran. Also, moose are routinely sighted just south of Jackson Lake Lodge along the Snake River and in the meadows fronting Jackson Lake, as well as in the meadows flanking the Moose-Wilson Road, a bucolic dirt road that is one of the prettiest drives in the park.

ELK (WAPITI)

No other sound in Yellowstone and Grand Teton portends the advent of changing seasons like the rapturous wail of a bull elk. Witnessing the breeding season, colloquially called the autumn "rut," is one of the most dramatic events for wildlife watchers in the Yellowstone region. The rut often involves sparring bulls locked in combat for the right to breed with elk cows.

Elk in the greater Yellowstone region form the foundation of successful wildlife watching because they are ubiquitous, numerous, and the epitome of majesty. Elk (*Cervus elaphus*) are the most abundant large mammal species in Yellowstone, numbering in the summertime more than 30,000 individuals and part of a regional population that is three times that number. About 20,000 elk remain in Yellowstone through the winter, the majority of them clustered in the northern grasslands.

The words "elk" and "wapiti," (pronounced WOP-it-tee) are used inter-changeably, for they refer to the same species. Wapiti, arguably the more poetic name, is a term handed down from the Shawnee Indians that means "white rump," a description that aids in their identification.

The subspecies of elk inhabiting Yellowstone and Grand Teton is known as the Rocky Mountain elk, a massive, widely distributed cervid native to montane forests and the subalpine foothills. At the end of the nineteenth century, elk had become an animal only found in the West, and even then they nearly disappeared from the Rockies because of overhunting. Market hunters killed elk for their ivory-like teeth, their meat, and to keep them off agricultural lands used by cattle ranchers.

Physically, elk are larger than deer but smaller than horses. Flaunting ornate, imposing antlers, bulls achieve weights ranging from 500 to 1,000 pounds, and stand over 5 feet tall at the shoulders. Cows, which do not grow antlers, weigh between 400 and 600 pounds.

An elk's head is darkish brown; the body from shoulders to tailbone is tan; and, of course, the rump is creamy white. Elk tracks resemble cloven half moons. Their droppings take the form of flattened piles similar to cow dung when the animals are eating succulent foods in summer, but it changes to pellet form during the months when they subsist on browse and drier food.

During the summer, elk disperse widely across Yellowstone and the national forests adjacent to Grand Teton. In September and October, the behavior of wapiti changes with the breeding season. Bulls emit high-pitched "bugles," adding a brassy sound to the parks that is as colorful as the changing leaves.

Stomping their hooves and wielding antlers in furious combat, bulls demarcate their territory through sparring, with dominant bulls drawing more cows into their breeding "harem."

Although some hunters employ artificial calls to draw animals closer during hunting season in national forests, it is illegal in Yellowstone and Grand Teton to use calls to imitate the bugling of bulls. In the past, photographers and visitors have been charged and injured by bulls that mistake these calls for those of other wapiti.

After the rut, elk gather in migratory groups. They flow out of Yellowstone on ancient game trails established hundreds or possibly thousands of years ago. In November, Yellowstone's largest elk herd begins to collect on the park's northern range, where as many as 20,000 elk seek vegetation hidden beneath the snow.

Meanwhile, to the south in Grand Teton, thousands of elk emerge from the national forest and cross the park en route to the National Elk Refuge. Every winter, thousands of elk are fed supplemental feed to offset the loss of winter range because of development in Jackson Hole.

If it is a severe winter, one-fourth of the herd may not survive, but the high mortality rate benefits other animals in the ecosystem, namely bears, wolves, coyotes, ravens, eagles, and other scavengers that depend on winter-weakened elk as an important food source. Despite their size, elk are the main diet of wolves, and elk calves are prey for mountain lions and grizzlies.

When spring arrives, pregnant cow elk give birth, with the new mothers and calves coming together in "nursery groups" that afford protection against predators.

Never, under any circumstances, should you approach elk. In the wintertime, forcing an elk to flee could cause it to expend valuable fat supplies needed to carry it through the winter.

Where To Find Elk

During the summer, scan the park's high meadows. Elk congregate regularly along the Gibbon Meadow near Norris Junction, throughout the lodgepole pine forests to Elk Park, and farther north around Mammoth Hot Springs. Year-round, wapiti can be seen grazing in sagebrush meadows and on the green lawns at Mammoth. Mammoth is also an excellent venue for observing the ritual of bugling in September.

Keep a careful watch as you travel over Dunraven Pass, near the lower and upper geyser basins around Old Faithful, and along the Madison River between the west park entrance and Madison Junction. The Firehole River, particularly from the upper geyser basin to Madison Junction, is a favorite spot among wildlife photographers who hope to capture the rut.

Migratory elk herds are also seen in winter and spring along U.S. Highway 191, which passes inside the park between West Yellowstone and Big Sky.

In Grand Teton, elk disperse widely throughout the park during the summer months but begin to congregate in September and October as they move toward their winter home on the National Elk Refuge. Several thousand elk gather on the refuge, located between the town of Jackson and the national park. Wildlife watchers can take sleigh rides through the wintering herds for a nominal charge, and the proceeds help buy feed for the animals. You can buy tickets at the National Museum of Wildlife Art.

PRONGHORN (ANTELOPE)

During the nineteenth century, Western settlers immortalized pronghorn in the classic folk song, "Home on the Range." Although known to many people by their colloquial name—antelope—these high plains speedsters are as photogenic as they are fast.

Relatives of such fleet African species as gazelles, pronghorn (*Antilocapra americana*) are, in fact, the swiftest land animals to race across the interior West. They can reach speeds of 70 miles per hour and spring 20 feet in a single bound.

The size of the pronghorn herd in both parks has fluctuated widely and both exist primarily as isolated island populations. Before settlement brought houses, development, and barbed-wire fences to the Yellowstone River drainage and the valley of Jackson Hole, nothing impeded the movement of pronghorn to larger populations that spread out eastward from the Rocky Mountain front.

In Yellowstone, the number of pronghorn reached an all-time high of perhaps 2,000 at the turn of the nineteenth century, before it dipped toward extirpation in the 1920s and rebounded to several hundred today. The number of animals in Grand Teton is slightly larger.

When you examine these small, hooved quadrupeds, it becomes obvious why they are called pronghorn. They are handsome creatures whose symmetrical, spiked horns are striking on males (bucks) and hardly noticeable on females (does). Their brownish markings, combined with a white-streaked underbelly, neck, and rump, make them easy to distinguish from other large mammals in the parks.

To tell the sexes apart, look for horns longer than the ears and black hair on the face and neck area of bucks, which are generally taller (about 3 feet at the shoulder) than females. Bucks weigh between 110 and 140 pounds. The horns of does, if you're able to spot them, are shorter than the ears.

Preferring lower elevations and open, sagebrush savanna, pronghorn occupy terrain that is shared with deer and elk, particularly during winter, when many ungulates gather on the windblown grasslands that extend beyond Yellowstone into Paradise Valley. In Grand Teton, pronghorn range between the park, the Bridger-Teton National Forest, and the National Elk Refuge.

As late spring and early summer approach, females begin disappearing from view, finding isolated coulees where they can discreetly give birth to their young, often twins. A seasonal ritual of both sexes is the shedding of a bark-like sheath from their horns. This occurs in late autumn, following breeding. The chief predators of pronghorn are coyotes, raptors, and mountain lions.

Where To Find Pronghorn

In Yellowstone, bands of pronghorn congregate year-round near the park's north entrance and along the gravel road running one way between Mammoth and Gardiner. Be on the alert for hikers and mountain bikers on this road. The McMinn Bench area also provides a fine vantage for pronghorn watching, and the animals are often visible on the paved road between Yellowstone's Roosevelt Arch in Gardiner and the open meadows beyond the entrance gate.

In Grand Teton, a thriving pronghorn population can be viewed in the sagebrush meadows between the Gros Ventre River Road and the Antelope Flats Road on the east side of U.S. Highway 191/89.

MULE DEER

Ideally suited to the mountainous foothills, mule deer (*Odocoileus hemionus*) truly are the deer of the West. As you drive through both Yellowstone and Grand Teton, everywhere you go is mule deer country.

Although there is no precise count of the mule deer population, the combined count of "mulies" in both parks is easily several thousand strong. In Yellowstone, heavy winter snows push mule deer out of the high country toward lower elevation grasslands inside and outside the park.

Members of the cervid (deer) family, mule deer males (bucks) flaunt mostly symmetrical antlers that are shed late in the winter. The size of antlers is determined by the genetic makeup of the parents and by the availability of nutrient-rich forage. Female deer (does) do not grow antlers.

When trying to determine mule deer presence along the roadside, look for cloven half-moon tracks that range in length from 2 1/2 to 3 1/3 inches. Other clues include beds of matted grass where mule deer rest during the heat of the day. Mule deer scat takes the form of either pellets or matted piles and dark brown balls.

Nature has given these plant-eating animals sharp vision, to identify approaching enemies, and good speed. Three physical characteristics make the mule deer easily recognizable: its oversized, creamy-white ears; its ropy, black-tipped tail; and its unique way of jumping and landing on all four feet at once, a gait called "stotting."

While mule deer bucks are polygamous, they do not amass harems of females like their elk counterparts. Males lead a solitary life except during the rut, while females congregate in groups on the same winter range year after year. This gathering is called "yarding up."

The mule deer's physical size and preferred habitat further separate it from its smaller cousin, the whitetail. While whitetails thrive in lower-elevation agricultural valleys with human presence, mule deer are primarily a foothills species. Its muscular frame reflects the fact that its summer range may include steep mountain slopes as high as 10,000 feet. The primary predators of mule deer are mountain lions, wolves, coyotes, and grizzly bears, which prey on deer calves in the spring.

Despite the mule deer's reputation as a browser, its diet is complex. Mulies feed in mature Douglas-fir forests, but they are also creatures of the sagebrush flats. Studies have documented mule deer in the Rockies eating over 673 different species of plants. While less discriminating in their diet than pronghorn and bighorn sheep, mule deer may embark on foraging expeditions taking them 30 miles or more in a night.

In recent years, mule deer populations in the West have fallen into decline. Some biologists attribute this to interbreeding with white-tailed deer, loss of habitat, and competition with growing numbers of elk. At the end of the nineteenth century, Yellowstone served as one of the few sanctuaries for the species following a dramatic dip in mule deer numbers caused primarily by overhunting. Mule deer hunting is prohibited in both parks.

Where To Find Mule Deer

In Yellowstone, the Lake, Tower, and Mammoth areas have resident mule deer populations during most of the year. They also are spotted from the roadside on the southern shores of Yellowstone Lake near Grant Village, and on the lake's northern shores from Bridge Bay to Lake Butte. Occasionally, auto treks in the vicinity of Old Faithful and between the northeast entrance and the Blacktail Plateau will also yield sightings.

In Grand Teton, mule deer are spotted along the forest edge east of U.S. Highway 191/89 between Moran and Moose. Also look for mule deer grazing on the south-facing slopes above the town of Jackson and on the flats around park headquarters at Moose.

WHITE-TAILED DEER

When we think of deer in North America, most of us think of white-tailed deer. Whitetails (*Odocoileus virginianus*) are the most abundant deer species in the lower 48 states and are abundant in both the suburbs and rural woodlands.

Yet this popular deer has actually been late in coming to the Yellowstone/Grand Teton region, and some biologists say that the proliferation of whitetails could mean the eventual end of mule deer. When the species interbreed, the genes of whitetails win out.

In the West, whitetails are found primarily along rivers and streams flanked by deciduous (leaf-bearing) trees, such as cottonwoods and willows. They also are associated with farmland and have slowly colonized mountain valleys by following the riparian corridors.

To be sure, the whitetail is more socially gregarious and tolerant of humans than its larger mule deer cousin. White-tailed deer are smaller and leaner than mulies and are distinguished by their reddish brown coats, white underbellies, and tails that are brown on top but white on the underside. When the tails are raised, they have the appearance of waving white flags. Like mule deer, male whitetails grow antlers while females do not.

In Yellowstone, whitetails have slowly moved up Paradise Valley and have demonstrated a growing presence in the vicinity of the Yellowstone and Gardner rivers. Here, their range overlaps somewhat with mule deer, elk, and pronghorn. Historically, a small number of whitetails wintered in the riverine lowlands, but the species, according to biologists, was virtually extirpated by the 1930s. The disappearance of whitetails appears to have been caused by factors outside of Yellowstone's borders, including livestock grazing, land clearing, development, and hunting. Since that time, however, whitetails have demonstrated a keen ability to adapt to habitat disturbance and in fact they appear to thrive on it.

In Grand Teton, sightings of whitetails have been spotty. However, whitetails have slowly been moving into Jackson Hole from the cultivated farmland of Idaho and many believe it is inevitable that whitetails will exert a greater presence in the park's riparian areas along the Snake River. One limited factor for whitetails in both parks is the harsh winter conditions.

Where To Find Whitetails

In Yellowstone, whitetails are frequently spotted in farmers' fields roughly 20 miles or less north of the park, but they are seldom seen in the park itself. In recent years white-tailed deer have been spotted occasionally between Elk Creek and Tower Falls, a few miles from Roosevelt Lodge.

In Grand Teton, whitetails are rare but they are occasionally seen on the golf courses and agricultural fields around Jackson Hole.

BIGHORN SHEEP

Rocky Mountain bighorn sheep (*Ovis canadensis*) thrive in the Yellowstone high country where other animals have a difficult time making a living. Few species are better suited to the mountains of Yellowstone and the bouldered slopes around Jackson Hole. Despite their preference for rugged environments, these animals are surprisingly visible at certain places along the roadside. A few hundred bighorns inhabit Yellowstone's northern range, with a smaller number finding refuge inside the park's interior.

By their appearance alone, bighorns symbolize ruggedness. Males (rams) are easily identified by the classic C-shaped curl of their horns, while females (ewes) sprout tiny fingers of horn from the tops of their skulls. So subtle are these spikes that females are frequently mistaken for mountain goats.

Nimble-footed and built with a low center of gravity, bighorns can scramble across rock walls too steep for most predators or humans. They disappear in a blink, only to reappear on another cliff. The bighorn is one of several members of the bovid family, which includes bison, mountain goats, and musk oxen. In modern times, though, only sheep and bison have been native to the park.

The biggest threats to the survival of bighorn sheep are disease, predators, and loss of habitat. In 1981 and 1982, an epidemic of chlamydia (pink eye) swept through Yellowstone's bighorn population, leaving hundreds of sheep blinded. Many died as a result, though it appears that bighorn numbers have recovered.

Although highly social animals, bighorns usually separate into nursery bands of ewes, lambs, and subadults, while rams form groups among themselves.

Rams in Yellowstone and the Jackson Hole area are renowned for their fully developed horns, a prize coveted by sportsmen and poachers outside the park.

Of course, hunting is prohibited in Yellowstone and Grand Teton, but it has not deterred poachers from illegally killing trophy animals. Park visitors play an important role in preventing poaching by reporting any suspicious activity to rangers.

Where To Find Bighorn Sheep

In Yellowstone, the most promising vantage point for seeing bighorn sheep is along the slopes of Mount Washburn, which is accessible via Dunraven Pass. By late summer, motorists may observe bighorns clambering down the bouldering washes that drain the mountain near the roadway. Also, drive to the Chittenden parking lot on the northwest slope of Mount Washburn and hike to the manned fire lookout tower on the mountain's summit. The sheep have a high tolerance for human hikers and are readily seen. Remember, however, to stay on the road or trail at all times. This alpine environment is fragile, and damage to vegetation can be irreparable.

Other places for finding bighorns are in the vicinity of Tower Falls near Junction Butte and the cliffs near McMinn Bench between Mammoth and Gardiner. Ewes frequently congregate there to lamb before leading their brood in a westward migration to the backcountry around Electric Peak.

In Grand Teton, the best vantage points for spying bighorn sheep are actually found outside the park in the cliffs flanking the Snake River Canyon. Some bighorns have been extirpated from the Tetons by the bustle of climbers and trekkers, although sightings in the park are still made, however irregularly.

MOUNTAIN GOAT

From any vantage point within Yellowstone or Grand Teton, mountains are visible on the horizon. One might assume that both parks therefore would be excellent outposts for finding billy (male) and nanny (female) goats, which occupy other high-elevation wildlands such as Glacier National Park. In fact, mountain goats (*Oreamnos americanus*) are only occasionally seen in the high peaks of Yellowstone and never in Grand Teton. At least not yet.

Mountain goats have brawny frames. They are sure-footed, with long, yellowish white fur and black, spiked horns. In fact, some people say the profile of the mythological unicorn was modeled after mountain goats. Males stand about 3 1/2 feet high and weigh between 120 and 250 pounds, while the females, which also have horns, are slightly smaller.

Based on the discovery of fossil remains found near Palisades Reservoir in Idaho and at paleoindian sites south and east of Yellowstone, goats may have lived near the park about 10,000 years ago, but then dispersed.

For hunting purposes, state wildlife officials transplanted mountain goats back into the region a number of years ago. Some descendants of those reintroduced animals have begun migrating into Yellowstone.

"During the past thirty years, one to fifteen goats have been reported at least seventeen times in the park, and on five occasions near the park," wrote former park research interpreter Norman Bishop in 1990. "Of the seventeen in-park observations, six were in the northwest corner and eleven were in the northeast corner of the park."

It may not take long before goats gain a permanent foothold in Yellowstone and no one knows when, or if, viable populations of goats will establish themselves in Grand Teton.

Where To Find Mountain Goats

In Yellowstone, seeing a goat is a rare event. The northeast corner of the park, on the cliffs flanking Baronnette Peak (north of the highway) and Abiather Peak (south of the highway), provide the best opportunities. If you see a goat, write down the location and report it to a park ranger.

BIRDS

BALD EAGLE

Bald eagles are not only our national wildlife symbol, but these great raptors, now on the conservation comeback trail, are lofty reminders of wildness in our national parks.

On June 20, 1782, Congress declared the bald eagle America's emblem of freedom by having the bird's silhouette placed on the Great Seal of the United States. Over the objection of Benjamin Franklin—who preferred the wild turkey—the eagle won the hearts of politicians.

The bald eagle (*Haliaetus leucocephalus*) adds a majestic quality to wildlife watching in Yellowstone and Grand Teton, reminding all park visitors that the boundaries of a living, thriving ecosystem do not stop on the ground. Eagles force us to look skyward, and to understand that the noble goals of habitat protection extend to the clouds where eagles soar and to the waterways where they hunt for food.

There are two eagle species in Yellowstone-Grand Teton, the easily recognizable bald eagle and the more land-hunting golden eagle, both of which are diurnal (day foraging) birds of prey.

As raptors, eagles seek out a protein-rich diet of fish, waterfowl, rodents, and small mammals, and scavenge the carcasses of megafauna such as deer and elk. In other words, they eat meat.

Despite their appearance, bald eagles are not really bald. Their name is derived from the Greek word *leucocephalus*, meaning "white-headed." The distinctive crown and tail feathers of a bald eagle take on their snow-white tint only as the bird reaches adulthood. That process may take four or five years and involve five different molts (feather sheddings) before the bird assumes its famous plumage. In the meantime, those unfamiliar with marking may mistake bald eagles for golden eagles, because both are adorned with brown feathers.

Complementing their white markings, bald eagles have yellow eyes and a prominent, hooked yellow beak. While males and females have similar plumage, the females are usually larger. Adult balds of either sex attain wingspans of 6 to 7 feet, giving them an imposing presence in the sky.

Eagles attract attention by virtue of their physical stature rather than any vocalization. When not flying, bald eagles seek out a prominent

perch, often in the tallest of pine or cottonwood trees, from which to scout their surroundings. In a standing posture, they are 2 1/2 to 3 feet tall.

It's natural to assume that Yellowstone—the world's first national park—or Grand Teton are idyllic settings for eagles, given their peerless setting and isolated locations. In Yellowstone, the park ornithologist places the number of adult nesting pairs at more than 15 but less than 30.

In Grand Teton and larger Jackson Hole, which is circuited by the Snake River, the count is far higher. Several dozen eagles winter in the region.

Yellowstone's high-elevation topography is, at best, marginal for eagle reproduction, while the Snake River in Grand Teton is far more conducive to successful rearing of eaglets.

Bald eagles are endemic to this continent, yet this national icon was reduced to staggeringly low numbers in the lower 48 states as recently as the 1960s. Today, more and more bald eagle populations are healthy enough that they no longer need the protection of the Endangered Species Act. (They still receive protection under the federal Eagle Act).

Yellowstone's most important role for bald eagles may be its use as a seasonal feeding area for migratory eagles passing through in the spring and autumn. Several hundred eagles make a temporary stopover along the trout-rich environs of Yellowstone Lake and the Madison, Yellowstone, and Snake rivers on their way to wintering areas in the Pacific Northwest or the central-southern Rockies.

Where To Find Bald Eagles

In Yellowstone, visit the shores of Yellowstone Lake and look for bald eagles along the banks of the Yellowstone and Madison rivers. As cutthroat trout start spawning in the Yellowstone River during early summer, the stretch of highway from Fishing Bridge into Hayden Valley may be a productive place to begin your search.

In Grand Teton, bald eagles are regularly spotted over the lakes at the foot of the Tetons and far more routinely, on a daily basis, along the riparian corridor of the Snake River, which runs north to south through the heart of Jackson Hole. Eagles have in recent years nested in the vicinity of the Oxbow Bend and human activity during nesting season is kept to a minimum to ensure successful roosting.

GOLDEN EAGLE

Golden eagles, named for their brilliant golden head feathers, are slightly smaller in stature than their cousins, the bald eagles. As champions of the thermals, they soar like dominant raptorian giants, achieving primacy over the mountainous foothills and meadow.

Compared to all other birds of prey except bald eagles, golden eagles (*Aquila chrysaetos*) are enormous, with wingspans measuring between 5 and 7 feet across and they, too, possess powerful talons used to snatch rodent and small mammal prey.

While there are areas where habitat for golden and bald eagles overlaps in the parks, the birds generally assert claims to different niches and terrain. Unlike balds, which rely heavily on fish and carrion leftovers, golden eagles fit the true aerial predator model, launching dives with wings partially tucked as they stalk prey. Some intrepid dives take goldens to speeds in excess of 120 miles per hour.

Gifted with excellent eyesight, goldens can detect the slightest movement of a mouse while circling in the sky. Their strength enables them to make effortless turns in the breeze, propelled by leisurely tilts and glides.

While identifying golden eagles, look first to the color of the feathers, then to the head. From the ground, the outline of a golden resembles that of a hawk. A patch of white is visible on the fanned, grayish tail feathers and between the brown and gray of the wings. It may take four years and two or three moltings (feather sheddings) until the adult bird's full feather plumage appears.

The crown of the golden eagle appears golden while its eyes are amber like the bald eagle's. The beak, though, is tipped with gray.

In the interior West, many ranchers claim to have problems with golden eagles killing their sheep, but it is illegal to shoot eagles and they, of course, are strictly protected in the national parks.

Where To Find Golden Eagles

In Yellowstone, golden eagles are uncommon but they can be seen in the early summer, drifting aloft over Lamar Valley near the confluence of the Lamar River and Soda Butte Creek, as well as over the foothills of the Gallatin Range near the park's northern entrance. The transitional landscape between river, sagebrush foothills, and mountains makes ideal habitat.

In Grand Teton, golden eagles soar above the sagebrush meadows east of the inner Teton Park Road and east of U.S. Highway 191/89.

OSPREY

Part acrobatic flyer, part angler, part indicator of clean water, the osprey is the least recognized raptor in Yellowstone and Grand Teton but among the most fun to watch.

Called "the fish hawk" by some, osprey (*Pandion haliaetus*) occur throughout the greater Yellowstone region. A sure sign of osprey presence is its classic bunch-stick nest built atop power poles or standing tree snags.

Osprey are found throughout the world but in Yellowstone and Grand Teton they adhere chiefly to backcountry lakes and riverine corridors where fish are abundantly available.

It is easy, at first blush, to mistake osprey for eagles but foremost they have "hawk" rather than "eagle" heads. In identifying osprey, take note of the marbled white head feathers, mottled brown-white wings, and patch of white on the breast. You may also notice the striped pattern on the tail.

Where To Find Osprey

In Yellowstone, osprey are commonly spotted gliding through the Grand Canyon of the Yellowstone River, along the shores of Yellowstone Lake and Lewis Lakes, and river corridors like the Madison. At last count, there were roughly 60 pairs of nesting osprey in Yellowstone.

In Grand Teton, the Snake River corridor, which supports dozens of nesting pairs of osprey, provides idyllic habitat for this fishing bird of prey. Park visitors who embark upon scenic floats of the Snake are often treated to osprey sightings. They also can be viewed along the shore of Jackson Lake along the Teton Park Road.

RED-TAILED HAWK

Red-tailed hawks are common throughout the wide-open spaces of the West and are frequently sighted soaring over sagebrush meadows or occasionally standing on fence posts along the roadside.

Red-tails (*Buteo jamaicensis*) are less timid around humans than other birds of prey. More research on red-tails is needed in both parks, but scientists say that red-tail numbers fluctuate in relation to the presence of available prey.

Wildlife watchers in Yellowstone and Grand Teton will see them most often in the river valleys where there is an abundance of mice, voles, and ground squirrels. In 1988, forest fires swept through Yellowstone, opening a dark canopy of lodgepole pine to a profusion of new plant life and a corresponding explosion in the number of plant and seed-eating rodents. That's why you should expect to see some red-tails on the edge of former forest burns.

While flying, red-tails reveal a classic hawk profile, with wings that extend more than 3 feet across and a fanned tail. The coloration is distinct. There are brown feathers on the head and rimming the outside tips of the wings. In a standing position, the red-brown tail is visible, as is the dark brown plumage and the yellow talons.

Where To Find Red-Tailed Hawks

In Yellowstone, red-tails are spotted often in the sagebrush meadows extending from park headquarters at Mammoth Hot Springs to the Tower-Roosevelt area and eastward into the Lamar Valley.

In Grand Teton, you will see red-tails along the inner Teton Park Road and along U.S. Highway 191/89 running between Jackson and Moran. In particular, the National Elk Refuge and the sagebrush meadows sprawling across the eastern half of Grand Teton offer good red-tail habitat.

PEREGRINE FALCON

The peregrine falcon's plight reminds us how fragile the web of life can be. But it also shows us the huge rewards that accompany wildlife conservation.

An efficient and ferocious avian predator, the peregrine (*Falco peregrinus*) can tear through the air like a bullet to snatch its principal prey, a duck or songbird or, in an urban environment, a common pigeon.

The precipitous decline in peregrines, which resulted in their eventual listing under the Endangered Species Act, was caused by widespread use of the pesticide DDT and habitat fragmentation. While DDT was toxic to insects and small mammals, the effect on raptors like peregrines and bald eagles was more insidious. The chemical entered the birds' bodies through secondary ingestion. Eggs from females became so brittle or thin-shelled that young could not develop. Thus, with poor reproduction, peregrines were cast into a downward population sink.

According to federal biologists, the peregrine was on the verge of extinction east of the Mississippi River by 1960, and ten years later the same fate awaited those birds in and around the Yellowstone ecosystem. The grim prognosis prompted calls for the peregrine to be listed as an endangered species in 1969, three years before DDT was banned.

Through support from the federal government and the nonprofit Peregrine Fund, based in Boise, Idaho, peregrine falcons are now quickly reclaiming their old niche and the species, nationally, appears to be biologically recovered. Over 500 birds were hacked (released) in the Greater Yellowstone area between 1980 and 1991, and at least 75 breeding pairs were established in the wild.

Both Yellowstone and Grand Teton contain excellent falcon terrain, and peregrines are routinely sighted by ornithologists. Peregrines can be identified by their intense features—black feathers that resemble a helmet on their head, pointing "falcon" wings and tail, and a light gray chest streaked with dark gray markings. When the bird is sitting, fuller dark gray feathers are visible on its back.

Despite its potency as a predator, the peregrine is relatively small, attaining an average adult wingspan of just over 3 feet. Falconers admire the peregrine for its ability to hunt and reach speeds of 200 miles per hour.

The outlook for peregrines, thanks to vigilant conservation, is bright in both parks, but don't expect to see many peregrines from the roadside. While they have become popular fixtures of the urban skyline, sailing between skyscrapers, they are creatures, especially during nesting, that need seclusion.

Where To Find Peregrine Falcons

In Yellowstone, scan the cliffs in the northeast and northwest corners of the park, and the more rugged areas of Hayden Valley west of the road.

In Grand Teton, look for peregrines in the craggy front of the Teton Range where meadow meets mountain and also in eastern sections of the park near the foothills of the Gros Ventre mountains.

GREAT GRAY OWL

Great gray owls (*Strix nebulosa*) are diurnal, haunting the forested meadows day and night, which means with a little luck wildlife watchers attuned to their movements have a good chance of seeing them. In Yellowstone and Grand Teton, where these avian hunters are probably more common than they seem, the majority of owl sightings occur around dawn and dusk.

At home in middle elevation coniferous forests, the great gray is one of the largest owls in North America, sporting a wingspan nearly 3 feet across. To ensure that there is plenty of wing clearance when it flies after prey, the great gray hunts on the edges of meadows and areas burned by forest fires.

Males and females look alike, and ornithologists say it's not unusual to find great grays foraging in pairs, which makes them easier to spot. Nonetheless, sighting them along the highway is difficult. It is best to simply pull over at a promising viewing area, turn off the car, get out, listen, and scan the meadowed edges with binoculars.

The great gray owl has a classic owl shape—an elliptical "face," protruding concentric patterns around the eyes, and a puffed and feathering mottled gray frame. Its feathers, of course, are predominantly gray, though streaked with white and brown. Even if you don't see an owl, you may hear it calling from the trees. When the owl vocalizes, it emits the stereotypical "hoo, hoo," sound. Native Americans have traditionally associated the owl with good omens and bad. In the national parks, seeing a great gray more often means an auspicious moment.

Where To Find Great Gray Owls

In Yellowstone, look for great grays in the meadows south of Canyon Village, and in the areas of formerly burned forest northwest of Roosevelt and Tower Junction near the Blacktail Plateau.

In Grand Teton, scan the forested meadows southwest of Moose along the dirt Moose–Wilson road and in the patches of forest and meadow along the Teton Park Road from Cottonwood Creek to the Signal Mountain road.

AMERICAN WHITE PELICAN

In 1863, nine years before Yellowstone was set aside as the country's first national park, an explorer was wandering the northern shores of Yellowstone Lake and spotted a clumsy-looking bird paddling a tributary. After the man raised his gun and pulled the trigger the name Pelican Creek was born.

You know a pelican when you see it. American white pelicans (*Pelecanus erythrohynchos*) are gregarious creatures whose oversized bills and frequent, awkward flapping and squawking make them favorites among birders and avian photographers.

The pelican, of course, is endowed with a long orange bill that helps it catch and shovel fish from the waterways it inhabits. As the name implies, the bird's plummage is white, though a gentle dusting of black feathers can cover the top of its head. As the pelican flies overhead, you may also notice the black primary and secondary feathers on the backs and tips of its wings.

During the spring trout spawn, you may see pelicans netting more than one fish at a time, holding them in a throat patch known as the gular, then swallowing the catch whole.

White pelicans are common in Yellowstone Lake and along the outflowing Yellowstone River. Park visitors eagerly form their own flocks near pelican feeding areas, but observation of pelicans should occur only from a distance, as the birds are easily disturbed, especially during nesting.

Between 200 and 400 pairs of pelicans nest in Yellowstone during the summer months, but the number can fluctuate depending on water levels in Yellowstone Lake. When melting snow and rain flood the lakeshore, hundreds of pelican eggs can be lost, but when the weather is less inclement and predation by coyotes and other predators is low, the peak population of pelicans in the park may swell to as many as 1,000 birds.

Migratory flyers, pelicans return each spring to the park. Researchers suggest that the Great Salt Lake a few hundred miles to the south serves as a staging area for pelicans before their spring arrival. When the pelicans leave by late September, they migrate via the Great Salt Lake to winter havens along the coastlines of California and Mexico.

Pelicans are delightful to watch, but human attraction can leave them vulnerable, too. Always offer pelicans plenty of space and never approach a nest site. Not only can your presence cause an adult bird to flee the nest but human odors can leave behind a scent trail for scavenging coyotes that might lead right to a nest or pelican fledgling. Fortunately, most pelican rookeries are located offshore on islands in Yellowstone Lake that are inaccessible to predators and people.

Where To Find American White Pelicans

In Yellowstone, the northern shores of Yellowstone Lake, the Yellowstone River where it passes beneath Fishing Bridge, and some of the smaller tributary creeks are the best places to spot pelicans from May through September.

In Grand Teton and vicinity, a healthy population of white pelicans can be viewed seasonally along the Oxbow Bend of the Snake River west of Moran and upstream on the Snake below Jackson Dam. They also can be seen on Flat Creek which flows through the National Elk Refuge. The birds make stopovers here in the spring during their migration to Yellowstone and in the late summer as they head south to their winter ranges.

GREAT BLUE HERON

Great blue herons (*Ardea herodias*) are quintessential water waders, strolling on their long, stiltlike legs through shallow pools or shores where minnows, frogs, and aquatic forage are available.

Herons are far more common across North America than sandhill cranes, and Yellowstone straddles the edge of the heron's range in the Rockies. Adult herons stand almost 4 feet tall, about 25 percent taller than adult sandhills.

The most efficient way to distinguish herons from cranes is to focus on shape, color, and habitat. Foremost, you will more often find herons in the water and cranes on dry land foraging in moist meadows or agricultural fields. The more robust herons are storklike in appearance, maintaining an S-shaped neck while either standing or flying. The heron also has a long, golden gray-blue bill, and a stringy plumb of feathers extending from its neck over the breast area.

This plumb was once highly prized by market hunters who sold the feathers to Eastern hat makers. As the bird's name connotes, the great blue's feathers are bluish gray, highlighted by black patches on the top of its head, at the base of its neck, and on its abdomen. White-tinted feathers are present beneath the bird's yellow eyes, along the front curve of its neck, and down the middle of its abdomen. Males and females are similar in appearance.

Herons nest in trees, usually beyond reach of coyotes and other predators, except for humans. Visitors who are caught disturbing nesting birds can be fined.

Where To Find Great Blue Herons

In Yellowstone, great blue herons are common along the rivers, especially the Madison River around Seven Mile Bridge, the Yellowstone River downstream from Fishing Bridge, and the Yellowstone River downstream from the town of Gardiner.

In Grand Teton, great blue herons are prolific along the Snake River and can be seen wading the shallows of Flat Creek where it flows through the National Elk Refuge.

SANDHILL CRANE

Like great blue herons, sandhill cranes (*Grus canadensis*) are masters of subtlety. The size and apparently awkward construction of these gangling birds might lead you to believe they lack the coordination necessary to make long flights or survive in the rugged subalpine environment of Yellowstone. But their appearance disguises their agility.

Lifting slowly off the ground, sandhills appear to painstakingly pull themselves to flight. Once airborne, however, they accelerate into effortless, balletic glides. General similarities in shape cause wildlife watchers to mistake sandhills for great blue herons, but upon closer examination they are distinctly different.

While sandhills and great blues are occasionally found in similar habitat, they usually thrive in different ecological niches. Sandhills, classified as "game birds" under some state waterfowl regulations, often prefer to plant their knobby-kneed legs on dry, solid ground. Herons, on the other hand, gravitate to calm and tranquil water. The calls of cranes and herons also differ. Cranes emit a sonorous "kroo" and "garoooo-ahh" while herons issue boisterous and curt "graaaks." Adult sandhills, which stand 3 to 4 feet tall, are predominantly light gray in color, with a willowy frame and a long, narrow neck held slightly bent. A crane's head is adorned by a noticeable patch of red over the eyes and crown, with a dark bill far smaller than a heron's. The body plumage of some adult birds may assume a reddish hue, due to the iron oxide soil transferred onto feathers when birds preen.

In flight the crane's body is fully extended, from its bill to the end of its nonwebbed feet. Sandhills, though smaller, are similar in appearance to their rare cousin, the whooping crane. In fact, sandhills have been used as surrogate parents to roost whooping crane eggs in an attempt to restore a natural population of whoopers to the wild.

Female sandhills, which are identical in appearance to males, will build their nests in meadows temporarily submerged by spring rain and melting snow. If the nests are not disturbed by humans or predators, as many as three eggs may hatch, producing young that fledge later in summer and join adult birds in leaving Yellowstone by mid-autumn.

Although there is a small breeding population of sandhills in the Yellowstone–Grand Teton area, it's uncertain how many of the birds inhabiting wetlands along the roadsides are transient. During the summer, sandhills fly back and forth from sanctuaries well beyond the parks. Park ornithologists say that several hundred cranes may pass through the parks seasonally in addition to a few dozen nesting pairs.

The sandhills you see in greater Yellowstone are long-distance flyers, spending the cold winter months in Mexico, Texas, and the Southwest.

Where To Find Sandhill Cranes

In Yellowstone, cranes can be spotted off Fountain Flats Drive near the Lower Geyser Basin and on the Swan Lake Flats south of Mammoth Hot Springs. Also look for sandhills that sometimes gather near Obsidian Creek in Hayden Valley.

In Grand Teton and vicinity, sandhills have been seen inside the National Elk Refuge and along the Gros Ventre River Road in the national park.

TRUMPETER SWAN

The sight of a trumpeter swan (*Cygnus buccinator*) breezing over a misty water surface while in wing-locked flight is regal and unforgettable. This swan, native only to North America, commonly leaves both poets and wildlife watchers smitten.

The trumpeter swan is another conservation success story with ties to the greater Yellowstone region. Once in a spiral toward extinction south of Canada, the trumpeter has made a comeback in the northern Rockies. A visitor to both Yellowstone and Grand Teton national parks may catch a rare glimpse of these snow-white marvels.

Trumpeters are the largest waterfowl in the world, and easily the biggest flyers in Yellowstone. Native Americans and early European explorers were drawn to trumpeters by the distinctive "koh-hoh, koh-hoh" vocalizations.

The wingspan of males (cobs) can reach 7 feet across, and though females (pens) are smaller, their beauty is no less profound. Cobs weigh between 25 and 30 pounds, while pens weigh slightly less.

Most wildlife watchers will recognize trumpeters by their elegant form. They are long-necked and entirely white except for their black bills and webbed feet. Unlike their domesticated cousin, the mute swan commonly found in urban parks, trumpeters swim with their necks only slightly curved. Despite their sometimes frail appearance, trumpeters are hardy, capable of enduring winter temperatures that reach 40 to 50 degrees below zero Fahrenheit.

The survival of trumpeters is one of storied success. By the middle of the nineteenth century, market hunters had almost completely killed off trumpeters from coast to coast. Ironically, the attractive plumage that makes these birds a joy to observe nearly led to their demise, as birds were slaughtered by the thousands to provide feathers for high-fashion hats. It appeared the trumpeter might be lost forever.

Miraculously, a small population survived in the isolated waters of the greater Yellowstone region. Yet by the 1930s, fewer than 50 were identified by federal biologists, all that remained from the tens of thousands that inhabited lower North America. An alarm was sounded in Congress, and soon the Red Rock Lakes National Wildlife Refuge west of Yellowstone National Park was set aside to facilitate trumpeter swan recovery efforts.

Although the region's trumpeter population has undergone population swings in the years since that refuge was created—with declines attributed to bad weather, threatened habitat, poisoning, collisions with power lines, predation, and disease—swan numbers now appear to be stable.

In recent years, the National Park Service has taken measures to reduce trumpeter deaths, including a program to ban lead fishing sinkers (which are toxic to birds), making sure there are no power lines in trumpeter flight paths, and reducing human impacts on nesting sites. Visitors play an important role in protecting swans by affording them space and staying clear of nesting sites.

Where To Find Trumpeter Swans

In point of fact, the best habitat for swans in the Yellowstone region is not inside Yellowstone National Park but on the lowland waters west of the park, which remain free of ice during the harshest winter conditions. Each autumn, wildlife watchers see hundreds of trumpeters gather in Yellowstone before settling upon the Henrys' Fork of the Snake River and the waters of Red Rock Refuge.

In Yellowstone during the spring, summer, and fall, you may find swans near the Seven Mile Bridge on the Madison River, on the appropriately named Swan Lake south of Mammoth Hot Spring, and along the Yellowstone River between Fishing Bridge and Canyon Village.

In Grand Teton and vicinity, look for trumpeters on Flat Creek, which flows through the National Elk Refuge.

CANADA GOOSE

For eons, Canada geese (*Branta canadensis*), also known as "Canada honkers," have sounded their way across the flyways of North America. Passing overhead in V-shaped squadrons, these hardy members of the duck family are abundant in most subalpine waterways of Yellowstone and some stream sections of Grand Teton.

The goose's coloration is exact. Its oblong black neck is tipped by a black beak, but flared by a half ring of white running from beneath the eyes down under the throat. From the bottom of the neck, the wide body is grayish brown, with a black tail tip. The bird's downy underside has whitish feathers on the belly and tail.

Adult honkers stand about 3 feet tall and weigh between 8 and 15 pounds. Yellowstone and Grand Teton do not have year-round populations of geese because of the harsh climate. The geese you see are either summer residents that rest here or transients passing through on their migrations.

Where To Find Canada Geese

In Yellowstone, Canadas are common in Hayden Valley along the grassy banks of the Yellowstone River. You'll also find them in the Lower Geyser Basin along the Firehole River, north of Norris Junction along the Gibbon River, and in Lamar Valley along the Lamar River.

In Grand Teton, you will occasionally see Canada geese in the lakes that stud the foot of the Tetons and along the Snake River, but more often Canadas are present along Flat Creek, which flows through the National Elk Refuge.

SAGE GROUSE

Across the West, many populations of sage grouse (*Centrocercus urophasianus*) are in trouble because of conflicts with agriculture and habitat destruction. These birds are sights to behold. Even Lewis and Clark commented in their journals on the grouse's rangy, proud appearance.

Sage grouse are not present in Yellowstone, but in Grand Teton hundreds of wildlife watchers flock every spring to the runways of Jackson Hole Airport to observe the birds' mating ritual, called "strutting." Males gather to puff their feathers in an ornate display and dance like turkeys or peacocks in an attempt to command the attention of possible mates.

Although these birds are normally associated with lower-elevation sagebrush country, Grand Teton holds a remnant population that is protected inside the park boundary.

Males are the more colorful and largest of the sexes. Measuring about 2 feet head-to-toe and weighing as much as 10 pounds, males have a black throat and white chest, which protrudes during the communal mating ritual.

Where To Find Sage Grouse

During nonmating times of the year, sage grouse can be seen occasionally in the National Elk Refuge, in the open flats off the Gros Ventre River Road, and in southern sections of the national park around the airport.

GALLERY

PORCUPINE

The prickly pear of the mammal world, the porcupine (*Erethizon dorsatum*) carries some 30,000 quills in its quiver, and each barbed quill can deliver a stinging reminder that the animal prefers to be left alone. However, contrary to myth, a porcupine cannot "shoot" its quills at intruders. The surest signs of porcupine presence are their tracks—the front tracks show four toes with claws, while the back paws reveal five claws and the catlike feces the animal produces when it browses on the bark of trees. Porcupines are widely dispersed in the forests of Yellowstone and Grand Teton, and are common along stretches of highway that dissect stands of old-growth forest.

SNOWSHOE HARE

"A jackrabbit with feet the size of snowshoes." That's how one park ranger describes the snowshoe hare (*Lepus americanus*). It thrives in the wooded subalpine environment of Yellowstone and Grand Teton, where snowfall is measured in feet rather than inches, hence the utility of wide feet. The snowshoe, which is the prime staple of lynx, camouflages itself by taking on a cloak of white fur from October through March and then turns a brownish color in spring. Though ubiquitous in both parks, it is seldom seen in daytime.

BEAVER

The wildlife symbol of industriousness, the dam-building beaver (*Castor canadensis*) has the power to shape the future of small streams in Yellowstone and Grand Teton. Known as a busy logger with curved buckteeth, the beaver can be identified by its webbed hind feet, lush brown coat, and paddle-like tail. Beaver presence is indicated by dams, domed lodges partially immersed in water and tree stumps gnawed to a conical point. You'll find them hard at work around dawn and dusk. Beaver can be viewed along the Yellowstone and Lamar rivers in Yellowstone and in Grand Teton along the Snake River.

MUSKRAT

In a shallow pond setting, the muskrat's house—constructed of cattails, reeds, mud, and twigs resembles a miniature beaver lodge. In deep lakes or fast-flowing streams, the muskrat (*Ondatra zibethicus*) digs burrows into the shoreline using underwater entrances. A muskrat's tail is long and leathery. Its hind feet are webbed, but the front paws are equipped with claws used to grip plants, which make up most of its diet. Muskrats remain active in winter, and you're most likely to see them at dawn and dusk. Often muskrats inhabit the same ponds and waterways as beaver.

WOLVERINE

The largest member of the weasel family is the "street fighter" of the forest. A wolverine (*Gulo gulo*) will confront mountain lions or bears to protect its share of a carcass. The wolverine's brawny frame sits low to the ground, and it can weigh as much as 50 pounds. Sometimes wildlife watchers will take it for a small bear. Look for patches of light, grayish hair on the flat top of the wolverine's head, and a brown or yellowish streak down the back that extends nearly to the rump. Wolverine are so scarce in Yellowstone and Grand Teton that any observation should be reported to park biologists.

SHORT- AND LONG-TAILED WEASELS

Weasels (*Mustela erminea/Mustela frenata*) are a delight to watch. Pound for pound, they are nature's most formidable mammalian predators, weighing 8 ounces or less but preying on animals many times their size. Weasels, members of the mustelid "weasel" family, have long tubular bodies and long tails. Other members of this extended family include mink, marten, fisher, otter, and badger. Brown with light tan fur during the summer, the weasel begins molting late in the season, replacing its brown fur with a coat of white hair that serves as winter camouflage. Weasels are found along rivers in the edges between meadow and forest.

PINE MARTEN

The pine marten (*Martes americana*) is a member of the weasel family and has the weasel's classic shape but it is larger. A tree-dwelling resident of old-growth forests, it finds shelter under dark, coniferous canopies. Its brown fur was highly coveted by European fur trappers and indeed the marten is known as the North American sable. Although rare, marten are seen along the southern shore of Yellowstone Lake. In Grand Teton, pine marten have been spotted along Jenny Lake and Colter Bay in Jackson Lake.

MINK

Another and perhaps the best-known member of the weasel family, mink (*Mustela vison*) are present generally wherever there are muskrat or similar prey. Larger than the weasel yet smaller than the pine marten, mink measure up to 2 Ω feet long, with long tails and chocolate or reddish brown fur. The mink is a capable swimmer and lives in ground burrows. It is a solitary and mainly nocturnal animal, active throughout the year. Adults are bold and ferocious. Look for mink along most of the lower-elevation waterways.

FISHER

Fisher (*Martes martes*) are larger than pine marten and the largest mustelid possessing classic weasel features. In fact, a fisher looks like a giant mink. Adults can reach weights of 12 to 18 pounds and lengths of over 3 feet. Part climber, part swimmer, and part burrower, the fisher lives in untamed backcountry and is the rarest of the nine members of the weasel family found in greater Yellowstone. The ecosystem lies at the southernmost tip of fisher range, and you're not likely to see a fisher from the highway. Fisher have been spotted in the

Shoshone Geyser Basin of Yellowstone, along Lewis Lake, and near the northeast entrance of the park. In Grand Teton, they have been seen in the vicinity of Jackson Lake.

BADGER

A badger's entire life is centered around digging—whether making its dens, escaping from enemies, or finding rodents on which to snack. The badger (*Taxidea taxus*) has a distinctive low, tank-like frame with muscular forearms, curved claws, and an irascible demeanor for uninvited guests. A vivid white line of fur runs the length of its snout, across its flat head, and along portions of the back. Patches of white between the eyes and the ears are ornamented by hooks of black. A marbled pattern of gray and brown covers the rest of its back and rump. You'll find badgers in the sagebrush meadows wherever there are thriving ground squirrel populations.

RIVER OTTER

Otters (*Lutra canadensis*) swim with poetry of motion. An oblong mustelid fond of blissfully spinning, tumbling, and swishing in the currents, the river otter is a wildlife watcher's favorite and frequently seen along the Yellowstone and Snake rivers. Otters are the largest swimming members of the weasel family. They are 3 to 4 feet long, with long, slender tails, webbed feet, grayish whiskers, and brownish bellies that are lighter than the rest of the body. You'll see them most often around dawn and dusk in Yellowstone Lake, along the Yellowstone and Lamar rivers, and in Grand Teton along the Snake River and in both Two Ocean and Emma Matilda lakes.

PIKA

As you hike through talus and rock outcroppings, you will probably hear pikas before you see them. Labeled "whistling hares," pikas have a closer resemblance to pet-show guinea pigs. The pika (*Ochotona princeps*) has reddish brown fur, wide, mousy ears, and white paws. It sounds a shrill, high-pitched bleat (or whistle) whenever it is threatened. In Yellowstone, the pika's bleat attracts not only humans but its predators, which include weasels and birds of prey. You'll find pikas at "the Hoodoos" between Mammoth and Golden Gate in Yellowstone and higher elevations of Grand Teton in mountain scree.

YELLOW-BELLIED MARMOT

Marmots and pikas share a similar ecological niche, haunting the higher elevations in rocky settings. The yellow-bellied marmot (*Marmota flaviventrus*) is also known as "the whistle pig" because of its chubby frame and the fact that it emits a screeching call when threatened by predators. Marmots are ground squirrel-like and surprisingly mobile. As the name suggests, they have fluffy, yellowish fur on their underbellies. Their backs are covered with gray-tinted hair that also has a tint of yellow underneath. They are common along higher-altitude sections of the highway.

LEAST CHIPMUNK

The least chipmunk (*Tamias minimus*) is found in coniferous forests where fallen logs or rock piles are present because these provide this tiny squirrel with safe places to flee from its mortal enemies, weasels and birds of prey. Although it doesn't hibernate in the more southerly regions of the Rockies, the chipmunk is driven into winter slumber here by the bitter cold and heavy snows that limit access to natural foods. Like most chipmunks, the least has classic black-and-white stripes running across its face and down its back, with orange hair and brownish tail. Like its larger cousin, the yellow-pine chipmunk, the least can be spotted at campgrounds throughout the parks.

UINTA GROUND SQUIRREL

This reddish gray ground squirrel shows little squeamishness around humans and knows how to entertain a crowd with its high-energy, jittery antics. Avoid feeding the uinta because habituating wildlife to human food often results in animals that cannot survive on their own and animals that turn aggressive and bite park visitors. The uinta (*Spermophilus armatus*) inhabits only a small section of the northern Rockies, and it spends seven months of the year in hibernation, longer than most other western ground squirrels or chipmunks. You'll find it along the boardwalks of Old Faithful, near Canyon Village, and at Mammoth. It is a favorite food for coyotes, badgers, and birds of prey.

HARLEQUIN DUCK

Harlequin ducks (*Histrionicus histrionicus*) are pretty rare but each year birders gather at Le Hardy Rapids in Yellowstone to record a sighting of these colorful waterfowl. The male harlequin's vivid blend of white, slate blue, and chestnut-hued feathers resembles the facial makeup of a circus clown, hence the name. These migratory ducks have a low tolerance for human intrusion upon their space, and their numbers have been in decline throughout the inner West. As a result, Le Hardy Rapids, one of the best harlequin viewing points in Yellowstone, has been subject to temporary spring closures to accommodate nesting ducks. Harlequins can also be found downstream along the Yellowstone River and along the Snake River in Jackson Hole.

BLUE AND RUFFED GROUSE

Separate species, blue grouse and ruffed grouse (pictured) inhabit different parts of the forest. Blues (*Dendragapus obscurus*) prefer high ridgelines in coniferous forests where they feast on juniper berries, grasshoppers, and other natural forage. The ruffed grouse (*Bonasa umbellus*) sticks to the lower deciduous forests of aspen, willow, and cottonwood. Blues are large by grouse standards, with bluish gray feathers on their back and necks and a slit of yellow near the eyes. Ruffed grouse are more mottled brown, with buffed feather patches and brown-and-white-streaked breasts. The ruffed engages in a wing-beating mating ritual called "drumming." You'll find blue grouse along Yellowstone Lake, over Craig, Sylvan, and Dunraven passes, and in Grand Teton around the vicinity of Signal Mountain and the Teton foothills. Ruffed grouse are present in the northern part of Yellowstone around the Gardner River near Mammoth and in Grand Teton along the Gros Ventre and Snake rivers.

COMMON RAVEN

Talkative and seemingly irreverent, ravens (*Corvus corvax*) respond to intruders (such as hikers) with a screaming "krraakk-kra!" Members of the crow clan, they pervade all developed areas of Yellowstone and Grand Teton, playing dual roles as beggars and as predators of insects, small rodents, songbird eggs and chicks, and even frogs. More than 2 1/2 feet tall, the raven is distinguished by its dark black feathers and long beak. You'll find these birds near most picnic areas and campsites. Resist the temptation to feed them when they come a-calling.

Where to Look When You're Out of the Car: A Few Favorite Walks and Hikes

Going on a wildlife watching safari in your car has its advantages. You can cover plenty of miles without being deterred by inclement weather, and your vehicle is a safe, comfortable, wildlife-viewing platform. However, the real magic of Yellowstone and Grand Teton lies away from the highways where natural sights and sounds are imbued with native scents and a more intimate physical connection to the landscape. In these places Yellowstone truly loses its comparison to a drive-through zoo. We encourage you to get out and walk, stretch your legs and your imagination. The following is a list of short hikes for wildlife watchers:

In Yellowstone:

Boardwalks in the Upper Geyser Basin .

Although most people visit the Upper Geyser Basin to watch the eruption of Old Faithful and other geysers, veteran wildlife watchers know the basin's boardwalks provide plenty of opportunities to see animals and use the thermal landscape as a dramatic backdrop for wildlife photography. Pick up a map of the area from the Old Faithful Visitor Center and proceed north toward Castle Geyser. Keep your eyes open as you look across the steam-filled meadows. In the morning and evening it's not uncommon to see a coyote, if not bison or elk, and even recently, wolves. Occasionally grizzlies amble through. On the far side of Old Faithful Geyser from the Old Faithful Inn, the trail leads to Observation Point and, beyond it, Solitary Geyser. The views from Observation Point across the Upper Geyser Basin are nice indeed. Bring your camera and binoculars.

Fountain Flats Drive and the Boardwalks in the Midway Geyser Basin.

When we choose to escape the huge crowds with our families, we head to Midway Geyser Basin. At Fountain Flats Drive, which winds near Midway Geyser Basin, you can drive to a parking lot, unload your bicycle if you have one, and continue to peddle along. If you don't have a bike, this is a great opportunity for a short hike. Elk and bison are regularly seen here as well as coyotes, and occasionally grizzlies and wolves. Keep your eyes open for raptors and remember not to feed the ravens.

Elephant Back Trail near Lake Hotel/Lodge.

A favorite hiking trail for park employees, the Elephant Back Trailhead is located about one mile south of Fishing Bridge Junction on the west side of the road. It climbs two miles to a wonderful overlook of Yellowstone Lake. In any season, grizzlies are frequently spotted and sometimes bison, moose, and elk.

Mount Washburn

There are two routes to the top of Mount Washburn, the rounded, 10,243-foot peak just to the north of Canyon Village. One trail is on the south side of Dunraven Pass, the other on the north. The trail on the south side is less busy and will get you to the top of Mount Washburn in less than four miles, one way. Both trails almost always give birders access to gray jays and Clark's nutcrackers, the latter of which are especially drawn to whitebark pine seeds that ripen in the autumn. During the warmer months, Mount Washburn is home to grizzlies that prowl the slopes, feeding upon plant stems, roots, and whitebark pine seeds. Always carry your bear pepper spray. The star inhabitants of Mount Washburn are the bighorn sheep; a resident herd is often visible as you near the top. Scan the ridgelines with your binoculars.

Lone Star Geyser near Old Faithful

The trail to Lone Star Geyser, one of the hidden geothermal gemstones, begins along the road on the northeast side of Craig Pass (the road connecting Old Faithful with West Thumb). Park your car in the lot and take the two and one-half mile trail to Lone Star. Occasionally elk are present and sometimes mule deer, but also look for Clark's nutcrackers and possibly grizzlies.

Bunsen Peak

Once you begin driving south out of Mammoth, you'll climb through switchbacks, then past the Hoodoos and Rustic Falls. A short distance later, once you drive out of the canyon, you'll see the parking lot for the Bunsen Peak trail. The route to the top is only two miles but you climb 1,300 vertical feet. Bunsen Peak offers commanding views of Mammoth Hot Springs and you may see a black bear, elk, or bighorn sheep.

Beaver Ponds Loop Trail

This route begins in Mammoth at the trailhead between the famous Liberty Cap thermal feature and one of the government buildings. The five-mile round trip climbs into meadows and forests and, especially in the spring and fall, often offers sightings of elk, mule deer, and coyotes, and sometimes bears and pronghorn.

In Grand Teton:

Jenny Lake and Hidden Falls

At South Jenny Lake Junction, park your car and take the boat ride across Jenny Lake to the trail for Hidden Falls, which is one and half miles further. Or, if you like, you can easily walk the three miles around the lake. Elk, mule deer, and black bear have been seen along the trail.

Phelps Lake

The Moose-Wilson Road (closed in winter) is one of the prettiest bucolic drives in the national parks. As you drive north you'll see the trailhead for Phelps Lake on your left. This is the trail to Death Canyon but, instead, plan on hiking a shorter distance and picnicking along the shore of Phelps Lake. Elk, mule deer, and bears have been seen in the Douglas-fir forest, along with a variety of birds such as ravens and Clark's nutcrackers.

So You'd Like To Know More?

The following organizations provide a wide range of educational services, including books and classes on a number of wildlife subjects.

Yellowstone Association

Founded in 1933, the Yellowstone Association is committed to assisting the public in all matters of natural history education. From membership fees and sales of books at visitor centers, the Association raises funds that are directed toward better interpretive programs on wildlife, geology, and the cultural history of Yellowstone. For membership in the Association or for more information, write: Yellowstone Association, Yellowstone National Park, WY 82190.

Yellowstone Institute

For wildlife watchers interested in learning more about specific animals in the national park, the nonprofit Yellowstone Institute offers a variety of field courses, including some that can be used to accrue academic credit. Located at the old Buffalo Ranch in Lamar Valley, the Institute presents both resident and day programs for modest fees. To obtain a course catalog, write: Yellowstone Institute, Yellowstone National Park, WY 82190.

Grand Teton Natural History Association

Like the Yellowstone Association, the Grand Teton Natural History Association is a world-class resource for information about Grand Teton National Park and the larger greater Yellowstone ecosystem. For the price of a membership, you will receive discounts on books, opportunities for field outings, and occasional lectures from visiting experts on wildlife, geology, and cultural history. For more information, write: Grand Teton Natural History Association, Grand Teton National Park, Box 179, Moose, WY 83012.

Teton Science School

Based at the eastern edge of Grand Teton National Park in scenic Jackson Hole, the Teton Science School offers renowned courses that explore the natural history of the Yellowstone ecosystem. For more information, write: Teton Science School, P.O. Box 68-B, Kelly, WY 83011.